C000131971

THE POET

GM 2

The Poet as Hero and Clown

A Study of Heym and Lichtenstein

Patrick Bridgwater

UNIVERSITY OF DURHAM 1986

© Patrick Bridgwater 1986
ISBN 0 907310 13 3

Contents

For Siegbert Prawer

Preface

It is, I think, little short of ridiculous that two such different poets as Heym and Lichtenstein have both come to be regarded as 'Expressionists'. In their lifetime they were considered opposites, and opposites is what they clearly are: the Prussian (Heym) and the Prussian Jew (Lichstenstein), 'Hellene' and 'August', poet-hero and poet-clown, tragic poet and satirist, rowdy and intellectual, poet of genius and poet of talent. As regards their work there is, similarly, a dichotomy between high-key poetry and low-key poetry, lyric/tragic poem and 'groteskes Stimmungsgedicht', tragedy and tragicomedy, inspiration and wit, passion and *gaminerie*. Of course, these distinctions are not absolute, for Heym is perfectly capable of writing scatological comic verses (though these were sports, not to be taken seriously), and Lichtenstein produced some romantic lyrics. That said, the distinctions are fundamental. Heym's poetry is as powerful as any ever written in German, the sort of poetry that is liable to reduce strong men to tears; Lichtenstein's poetry is more likely to make them laugh out loud, for he is a master of sly comedy. Heym, then, is an enthusiastic adept of the overstatement, Lichtenstein a master of the understatement. Heym used to read his poems at *Neopathetisches Cabaret* meetings, and was indeed regarded as the *Neopathetiker par excellence*; Lichtenstein was not even invited to read there. One cannot imagine Lichtenstein sitting at his writing-table wearing nothing but a Jacobin sash, for this was simply not his style; his forte was not the heroic gesture, but that most anti-heroic of all gestures — the satirical aside.

Since its rediscovery in the 1950s Expressionism has received too much critical attention in the sense that so much emphasis on the movement has, one can now see, been a positive hindrance to our understanding and appreciation of some of the major writers who have come to be grouped under the Expressionist umbrella. The poetry of Georg Heym and Alfred Lichtenstein is an example of this. What this brief study therefore seeks to do is to examine the poetic work of these two brilliant and very different individuals on its own merit. I am concerned neither to examine Heym's and Lichtenstein's relationship to poetic expressionism, nor to deny that such a relationship exists. My concern is simply to put the emphasis back where it belongs: on the poetry.

Acknowledgements

For permission to quote poems which remain in copyright I am most grateful to Kraus Reprint Co. (for Ernst Blass's 'Berliner Abendstimmung') and Verlag C.H. Beck (for Georg Heym's 'Widmung' and 'Die Hölle, I'). For good advice I am grateful to my colleagues Dr. J.W. Smeed and Dr. K.F. Hilliard. Kathleen's typing was as beautiful as ever.

I.   The Poet as Hero: Georg Heym

A Man Possessed

Georg Heym was born on 30 October 1887 at Hirschberg (now Jelenia Góra) in Lower Silesia. Most of the external facts of his life are irrelevant to his work; it is the natural phenomenon, the demon within, that counts, for Georg Heym was a man possessed. He began writing poetry in 1899; from December 1904 he kept a highly revealing diary. By the time he changed schools in April 1905 he had already written almost 90 poems, mostly nature-poems, some of them of a formal perfection that puts one in mind of the young Hofmannsthal. In all he wrote some 400 poems, 250 of which are 'early' poems, while the other 150 are the 'mature' poems to which he owes his reputation. His only non-posthumous collection, the ironically titled *Der ewige Tag*, appeared in 1911. On 16 January 1912 he was drowned under appalling circumstances. His second collection, *Umbra vitae*, appeared posthumously in 1912. The first, incomplete collected edition of his work, *Dichtungen*, came out in 1922; it has now been superseded by the *Dichtungen und Schriften* edited by the late K.L. Schneider. Now that he has lain graveward with his furies for well over two generations, it is high time that Heym received greater recognition, for there are few more eloquent and passionate monuments to 24 years of life than Heym's poetry.

He was an extraordinary young man: self-absorbed, lonely, obsessed with beauty, love, evil and death. At one stage one of his proudest possessions was an old skull which he crowned with a wreath of vine leaves. Foreseeing his own early death and its hideous nature, he had a passionate appetite for life. He longed for a life of infinite glory and was engrossed by the lives of men like Leonardo da Vinci, Hölderlin and van Gogh; he would have liked to live in the 5th century BC or during the Renaissance or at the time of the French Revolution. He envisioned a dramatic, heroic death: 'meinen Totenkranz in den Haaren möchte ich auf das abendliche Meer fahren. Es müßte dann gerade ein schöner Herbsttag sein': (*T:* 18.10.05). The diary contains other, similar versions of 'his' death; his ideal must have been the death of Leonardo da Vinci as described by Dmitri Merezhkovsky in *The Forerunner* (1902), which moved him to tears every time he read it — and he read it repeatedly; but he will also have noted and applied to himself the words spoken by Niccolò Machiavelli: 'My friend, there is naught more terrible than to feel in yourself the power to do something, and to know you will perish and die without ever having accomplished anything whatsoever.'[1] He identified with all his heroes, including Leonardo, for was not Leonardo the artist as Hero, a great artist, a great atheist, and indeed a man who, like Heym himself (under his influence ?), was given to finding chimerical monsters in the outlines of clouds? The gulf between heroic image of death and terrible reality — the only heroic thing about that was Heym's attempt to save his friend's life — reminds us that he once wrote that if God existed, he should be hanged for his infinite cruelty (*T:* 17.8.10). He was a pagan whose prayers were directed to Helios: 'Immermehr festigt sich . . . in mir der Glaube an Helios, an das Licht, die Sonne, das ganze heilige Weltall' (*T:* 14.9.06). He was a dreamer who lived for his dreams, which he cultivated to the point where they became visions. Like Trakl, he became possessed by these visions, becoming almost demented when he was unable, for one reason or another, to record them: 'Quälerei, Elend, die dichterischen Bilder rauschen mir aus den Ohren heraus, statt, daß ich sie zu Papier bringe' (*T:* 20.12.10). Seeing everything as 'grau in grau' (*T:*30.5.07), he needed a 'Lichtpunkt' (*T:* 24.5.05) to lighten his existence. No doubt this is why his prayers were directed to 'Helios'. His main source of light in this sense was beauty, in which he believed quite passionately: 'Ich glaube, es gibt keinen größeren Gott für uns, als die Schönheit' (*T:* 18.12.05), 'Ich kann es nicht sagen, wie ich die Schönheit liebe' (*T:* 13.8.06). He needed beauty as much as he needed love. His poetry is the product of a blessedly powerful imagination that needed to be fuelled by extreme feelings, although he wrote better on the down-beat of passion than on the up-beat; he is an *elegiac* love-poet of immense power. No one has charted the landscape of sorrow and loss more beautifully than Heym; at his best he is a marvellous poet, a poet whose words fork lightings. Central to his being and to his work is imaginative passion. He was frequently reduced to tears by the very vehemence of his feelings. He loved 'les extrêmes' and hated mediocrity in every shape and form. Niggardliness was not in his nature. His work is dramatic, emblazoned with images of death, but throbbing with life.

He was an out-and-out Romantic. He lived for love, 'die Liebe, die ewige, erlösende allbezwingende Liebe' (*T:* 16.12.06), and for the concomitant passion of creativity. He made a cult of love — 'Mir ist die Liebe sosehr Religion, wie wohl keinem' (*T:* 266.10.06) — and worshipped Woman well on the other side of idolatry: 'Ich bin geneigt, das Weib als Göttin aufzufassen' (*T:* 15.5.05). Being in love, or thinking himself in love, was for him a necessary condition; without it he would become melancholy, even suicidal. He had only to catch sight of a beautiful girl, to be quite carried away. He loved Hölderlin as much for the depth of his love for Diotima, as for the beauty of his tragic poetry; he envied him the depth of his experience, envied him the happiness of experiencing such deep sorrow! He dreamt of a 'grande passion', and if he experienced mostly 'kleine Liebeleien', this did not really worry him, for being in love mattered to him more than the object of his love ('ohne ein Mädchen, das ich liebe, kann ich nicht sein' — *T:* 10.3.05). He asked himself 'Bin ich einer derer, die die Liebe lieben, aber nicht den Gegenstand' [?] (*T:* 2.4.05), and in his heart he knew that he was. It was the idea of love that mattered. The girls with whom he was forever falling in love were more a part of his dreams than anything else. When he writes in his diary 'Doch er ging seinen Weg weiter. Da kam ihm ein Mädchen in den Weg, die schön war und seelengut. Und wieder flammte sein Herz auf' (*T:* 17.6.05), this is pure fairytale, the myth of *Brüderlein* and *Schwesterlein.* It was no doubt because, like Baudelaire before him (*pace* Apollonie Sabatier), he needed love more than he needed any given object of it, that his numerous *affaires de coeur* ended in disenchantment. Dreams alone are perfect. They are also hard to live up to; being a goddess takes it out of a girl.

This man's dreams were extraordinarily martial. He dreamt of military glory, of serving — and dying — with distinction in the armies of Napoleon, whom he idolized. His ideal was heroism in whatever form — in love, in battle, in death; but he was also a revolutionary and once said (in the days before terrorism became so banal) that one of his selves would have liked to be a terrorist. He was more than a youthful rebel reacting against the petty tyrannies of his father and of society, for he cultivated his revolt to the point where he could no longer conceive of himself without his Jacobin cap. On 3 August 1911 he wrote to Hildegard Krohn: 'Wäre ich doch in der französischen Revolution geboren. Heut gibt es nichts, für das man sich begeistern könnte, nichts, das man zu seiner Lebensaufgabe machen möchte, schlimmer als Pest und Cholera' (*DuS*, VI, 512). A few weeks later he went further: 'Ich sehe mich in meinen wachen Phantasieen, immer als einen Danton, oder einen Mann auf der Barrikade, ohne meine Jacobinermütze kann ich mich eigentlich garnicht denken . . . Mein Gott, wäre ich in der französischen Revolution geboren, ich hätte wenigstens gewußt, wo ich mit Anstand hätte mein Leben lassen können' (*T:* 15.9.11). He identified with Robespierre as well as with Danton. Not a few of his poems relate to the French Revolution. The picture of him sitting on the outside windowsill of David Baumgardt's flat in Charlottenburg singing the Marseillaise (*DuS*, VI, 11), is a startlingly vivid glimpse of the *real* Heym, as is the picture of him sitting writing poems like 'Ich verfluche dich, Gott' in front of an open window, wearing only his Jacobin cap and *écharpe.* His rage is ultimately more metaphysical than political.

Although there is no reason to suppose that he was aware of it, this revolutionary's basic philosophy was expressed in the famous 'Conclusion' to the first edition of Walter Pater's *The Renaissance:*

> *Philosophiren,* says Novalis, *ist dephlegmatisiren, vivificiren.* The service of philosophy, of speculative culture, towards the human spirit, is to rouse, to startle it to a life of constant and eager observation. Every moment some form grows perfect in hand or face; some tone

on the hills or the sea is choicer than the rest; some mood of passion or insight or intellectual excitement is irresistibly real and attractive to us, — for that moment only. Not the fruit of experience, but the experience itself, is the end. A counted number of pulses only is given to us of a variegated, dramatic life . . .

    To burn always with this hard, gemlike flame, to maintain this ecstasy, is success in life . . . While all melts under our feet, we may well grasp at any exquisite passion . . . we are all *condamnés*, as Victor Hugo says: we are all under sentence of death but with a sort of indefinite reprieve — *les hommes sont tous condamnés à mort avec des sursis indéfinis:* we have an interval, and then our place knows us no more. Some spend this interval in listlessness, some in high passions, the wisest, at least among 'the children of this world', in art and song. For our one chance lies in expanding that interval, in getting as many pulsations as possible into the given time. High passions give us this quickened sense of life, ecstasy and sorrow of love, political or religious enthusiasm, or the enthusiasm of humanity. Only be sure it is passion — that it does yield you this fruit of a quickened, multiplied consciousness. Of such wisdom, the poetic passion, the desire of beauty, the love of art for its own sake, has most. For art comes to you, proposing frankly to give nothing but the highest quality to your moments as they pass, and simply for those moments' sake.

Had he known it, Heym would surely have been delighted by this classical statement of a philosophy so close to his own. Every page of his diary records his determination not to 'sleep before evening' on this 'short day of frost and sun.' He, more than most men, had what Pater calls 'this sense of the splendour of our experience and of its awful brevity'; none knew better than Heym the 'pagan sentiment' which 'measures the sadness with which the human mind is filled, whenever its thoughts wander far from what is here and now.' He is a pagan not just in the sense of cultivating a pagan Hellenism, but in the sense of seeing what Pater calls the 'bewildering toils' of life in primitive, mythological form: in the form of demons. He would have recognized Pater's statement of the Epicurean creed for the counsel of perfection that it is and would, I think, have recognized — like Pater himself — the peril of such an Epicurean creed. By this I mean the fact that such a philosophy is purely self-regarding and involves, or at least does not preclude, the temptation of a gross indulgence in sensuous delights. Heym himself avoided neither of these dangers; but it is the poetic passion, the passion for beauty, that is the positive pole of his existence. He was in no doubt at all that 'Schönheit und Kunst dem Leben einzig Wert verleihen' (*T:* 6.8.06).

    He had a violently contradictory personality. It seems strange that such a furious rebel and zestful, exuberant individualist should also have been a 'poet of bile and brainstorm',[2] a 'poet of the most macabre visions and miasmic scenes',[3] but it is a fact that 'Heym's sombre meditations on death provide the foil to his yearning for glory, enjoyment, and triumph, his dream of a wild exuberant life in years to come. This brooding introvert is at the same time possessed by a fierce vitality, a hunger for love, experience, physical and emotional fulfilment'.[4] Heym himself comments on the struggle within him of the 'Seele des Lichts' and the 'Bierseele' (*T:*

22.12.05); he adds: 'In mir wechseln Begeisterung und Widerwillen, Glauben an mich und Verzweiflung an mir' (*T:* 31.10.06). Poets frequently suffer from a genial tension between self and anti-self; but they rarely combine introvert and extrovert in such a way or to such a degree. Heym himself was fully aware of what he called, in a phrase worthy of Hölderlin, 'diese unseelige Zweiheit in mir', adding 'Ich bin heut Tier und morgen Gott' (*T:* 16.7.05); he was alarmed at the extent of the division; indeed, shortly after this he noted in his diary 'daß ich aus 2 ganz verschiedenen Menschen bestehe' (*T:* 26.10.06). In 1910 we even find him writing of himself as three different people, 'Poet', 'Wahnsinniger' and 'Künder': (*T:* 5.11.10). He rather spoils the effect by misspelling 'Künder' as 'Kinder'!

His diary shows that he was always liable to slip from elation into wild sorrow. No doubt this violent oscillation between passion and spleen, ecstasy and despair, has a psychological explanation. Heym was himself morbidly aware of the relationship between what Sokel has well called his 'melancholy death-bound self' and his 'restlessly ambitious life-bound self'.[5] Paradoxically, the poet who produced some of the most violent poetic imagery ever was the most sensitive of individuals, ashamed of the delicacy of his own feelings, afraid to wear his heart on his sleeve for fear of being rebuffed or ridiculed. At times he felt that he was not a real person at all: 'Ich bin nämlich gar kein Mensch. Ich bin nur irgend eine Art Spiegel gewissermaßen, der anderer Menschen heiße Gefühle in sich aufnimmt und zurückstrahlt, aber eigene Gefühle kann ich mir nicht erlauben' (*T:* 20.7.06). He was, in other words, sometimes frightened of the vehemence of his own feelings. He illustrates, as well as anyone, the 'Disproportion des Talents mit dem Leben' of Goethe's Tasso, showing his awareness of the fact by noting in his diary 'Mir ist wenigstens gegeben, zu sagen, was ich leide' (*T:* 5.9.09). The apocalyptic mood which so many of his poems explore has a terrifying personal dimension; the horrors and unhappiness of his life make the most complete and hideous sense once one realizes him to have foreseen how it would end. In a general way he appears to have shared Nietzsche's view of art as the last metaphysical activity of man. A few months before his death he wrote: 'Man könnte vielleicht sagen, daß meine Dichtung der beste Beweis eines metaphysischen Landes ist, das seine schwarzen Halbinseln weit hinein in unsere flüchtigen Tage streckt' (*T:* 15.9.11). It is typical of him that the image (we shall see presently that it is a cloud-image) preceded the thought; it remains more significant. But this does not mean that he had any illusions about Art, for he also recorded his view that 'Die Dichtkunst . . . ist ein sehr kümmerliches Surrogat für die Tat und für das Leben' (*T:* 7.12.10). He would not have been Georg Heym if he had taken any other view.

Poetic Heroes

His diary also leaves us in no doubt as to the poetic heroes of his youth: 'Ich liebe alle, die in sich ein zerrissenes Herz haben . . . Ich liebe alle, die nicht von der großen Menge angebetet werden. Ich liebe alle, die oft so an sich verzweifeln, wie ich fast täglich an mir verzweifle' (*T:* 20.7.09). This caused him to idolize Hölderlin, Grabbe, Kleist, Büchner and Nietzsche; Keats, Shelley, Byron and Marlowe; Baudelaire, Rimbaud and Verlaine. This is not to say that these writers were all important influences on his work, although a few of them were. All were, however, men whose honesty or ability to cope with difficulties similar to his own he admired. He had no time for those whom he saw as compromisers, including Goethe (whom he calls a 'Kunstbonze im Nebenberuf' and an 'aufgeblasener Idiot und feister Wasserkopf' — *T:* 3.11.10), George (towards whom his attitude was ambiguous) and Rilke (that 'Spatz mit Pfauenfedern': *DuS*, III, 98), although he was himself both a little readier to compromise than he would have liked to think, and rather more indebted to Goethe, Rilke and — above all — George, than he would have dreamed of admitting. George he called not only 'die Binger tönende Pagode' (*DuS*, VI, 15), which is bad enough, but also 'tölpelhafte[r] Hierophant, verstiegene[r] Erfinder der kleinen Schrift und Lorbeerträger ipso iure' (*T:* 8.7.10), which is worse, and George is guyed in the satire 'November' (*L* 155): 'stefan george steht in herbstesstaat. / an seiner nase hängt der perlen helle'. But if there was much about George and the George-circle of which Heym naturally disapproved, there were also aspects of George's work which compelled his admiration, as even his use of the initial 'Des' (for 'Dessen') shows. Heinrich Eduard Jacob summed up Heym's attitude to George with admirable clarity:

> George — den er maßlos haßte, im Unbewußten aber vielleicht so sehr verehrte, wie Kleist Goethe gehaßt, verehrt und geliebt hatte — war für Heym eine Art von Ahnenschicksal. George nicht als Geist . . . und andererseits auch nicht das Georgesche Gedicht, das er in seiner ganzen Ausdehnung überhaupt nicht kannte — wohl aber George als Form, als Äußerung jenes Zwanges zur Latinität, den George selbst von Baudelaire übernommen hatte. Diese Form umschloß zeitlebens den Rasenden wie ein Kristall. (*DuS*, VI, 70)

Georg Heym was a man possessed, and knew it, as the poem 'Widmung' (*L* 105) shows:

Der du, ein Sturm, mich durchwanderst Tag und Nacht,
Der du in meines Blutes dunkelen Gängen wohnst
Der es brausen macht.

Der dunkel und rätselvoll,
Tief in mir thront.
Ungerührter, der mich zu schauen heißt
Wie nie ein andrer geschaut
Des Sommers Fluren, den Wald

Und die Städte,
Wenn dunkel der Abend graut.
Der du mich durch die Straßen reißt.
Der mein Herz zittern macht. Du.
Wie oft stand ich maßlosen Taumels voll
Wenn dein Fittich rauschte mir zu
'Den' Ton, den keiner vernahm.
Der du in meinem Herzen wohnst.
Wie lange noch?
Bis du ausfährst eines Tags,
Wie ein dunkeler Rauch,
Und mich verläßt,
Wie die bekränzte Tafel
Nach einem Totenfest.

Of course these are the lines of a young poet who has discovered Hölderlin, but they are none the worse for that; the 'Feierlichkeit' is entirely genuine and wholly justified. Who, under the circumstances, would not feel awe? Hölderlin was Heym's first poetic — and human — idol. In a diary entry he explains why: 'ich liebe ihn wegen seiner Schönheit, und daß er *des* größten Schmerzes geweiht wurde' (*T:* 10.9.05). In other words, his love of Hölderlin is explicable first and foremost in human terms: he idolizes Hölderlin for the searing passion of his life. It is, of course, *Liebesschmerz* to which he is referring; Hölderlin's love for Diotima is never far from his thoughts at this time. His deliberate *Hellenentum* is modelled on Hölderlin, but more generally what Hölderlin gave him was enthusiasm. At the same time a poem like 'Widmung' makes it clear that the late Hölderlin — the poet of, say, 'Hälfte des Lebens' — was his first poetic model and a formative influence, while a study of Heym's late poetry shows that he was returning to Hölderlin when death intervened. This is a point to which we shall return. For the present let us note that Heym's indebtedness to Hölderlin is not necessarily expressed in formal terms. There is another poem, 'Marengo' (*L* 165), written in December 1910, by which time Heym was under other formal influences, which I must quote because it is both steeped in Hölderlin and also illustrates Heym's imaginative preoccupation with the Napoleonic wars:

Schwarzblau der Alpen, und der kahlen Flur,
Die Südsturm drohn. Mit Wolken tief verhangen
Ist grau das Feld. Ein ungeheures Bangen
Beengt den Tag. Den Atem der Natur

Stopft eine Faust. Hinab die Lombardei
Ist Totenstille. Und kein Gras, kein Baum.

Das Röhricht regt kein Wind im leeren Raum.
Kein Vogel streift in niedrer Luft vorbei.
Fern sieht man Wagen, wo sich langsam neigt
Ein Brückenpaar. Man hört den dumpfen Fall
Am Wasser fort. Und wieder droht und schweigt
Verhängnis dieses Tags. Ein weißer Ball,
Die erste der Granaten. Und es steigt
Der Sturm herauf des Zweiten Prairial.

Walter Schmähling made an interesting point about 'Marengo':

> Hölderlin . . . schrieb 1800 den Entwurf zu einer Napoleonhymne *Dem Allgenannten*. In einer Strophe steht Napoleon (auch hier wird der Name nicht ausgesprochen) über den Alpen, 'Hinsehend über Italien und Griechenland — Mit dem Heer um ihn — Wie der Gewitterwolke . . . ' Es gibt wohl keinen Beweis dafür, daß Heym dieses Fragment gekannt hat. Aber das Sonett *Marengo* atmet Hölderlinschen Geist.[6]

The last sentence here makes my point: that 'Marengo' is the work of a young poet who is steeped in Hölderlin and shares his enthusiasms, the cult of Napoleon included.

A year later he has a new idol to place beside Hölderlin, 'den herrlichen Grabbe' (*T:* 31.10.06), and the reason is again a personal one: 'ich bin gewillt, wie Grabbe ein trostloses und jammervolles Leben zu führen' (*T:* 11.11.06). Then he finds another desperate Romantic hero: Heinrich von Kleist (*T:* 21.10.07). In 1905 he had quoted Hofmannsthal in his diary, evidently agreeing with him that it is 'viel zu grauenhaft, als daß man klage, / daß alles gleitet und vorüberrinnt', and in October 1908 we find him, like so many young poets of the time, paying Hofmannsthal the compliment of imitating him : 'Durch herbstliche Alleen . . . ' (*L* 665) is based on Hofmannsthal's 'Vorfrühling'. Two years later, by which time he is back in Berlin and has already given a reading at a *Neopathetisches Cabaret,* we find him recording his view that 'Ich glaube nicht, daß es einen größeren Lyriker gibt, als Keats' (*T:* 31.10.10). A week later he lists Keats together with Shelley, Baudelaire, Verlaine and Rimbaud (*T:* 5.11.10), and it is here that we come to two major influences, Baudelaire and Rimbaud, and a minor one, Keats. Before considering these influences, it is worth remembering that the friend with whom Heym was drowned, Ernst Balcke, was a student of English and French literature, and is said to have written poetry in French as well as German.

Heym may well have owed his enthusiasm for Keats to Balcke, who drew his attention to 'Isabella; or, The Pot of Basil' in October 1910. Keats clearly held his interest, for in June 1911 he wrote to Hildegard Krohn that he was on his way to Balcke's to talk about Keats (*DuS,* VI, 507). In his review of *Der ewige Tag* in May 1911 Balcke had commented that 'von der Dezenz, welche Keats im Basil-Pot bei der Schilderung des toten Lorenzo so unvergleichlich bewahrt, ist in seinen Gedichten nichts zu verspüren' (*DuS, VI,* 193), which may well have been what Heym wished to discuss. Be this as it may, it was evidently to Heym the romantic that Keats appealed, as is shown by the fact that we find him quoting from 'Isabella' the lines 'Love! thou art leading me from wintry cold, / Lady! thou leadest me to summer clime' in a letter to Hildegard Krohn. The effect on his own work of his reading of Keats is another matter. If one thinks of the sort of poetry that Heym was writing in 1910, much of it massively detailed, packed tight with images, it seems likely that he is following the example, in this respect, of both Keats and Baudelaire, for, as Arthur Symons once said,

'To load every rift with ore:' that, to Keats, was the essential thing; and it meant to pack the verse with poetry so that every line should be heavy with the stuff of the imagination . . . For as Keats, almost in the same degree as Baudelaire, worked on every inch of his surface, so perhaps no poets ever put so much poetic detail into so small a place . . . [7]

In the long run Baudelaire meant even more to Heym than Keats did. So did Rimbaud.

When Heym wrote 'Ich liebe alle, die in sich ein zerrissenes Herz haben . . . ich liebe Rimbaud' (*T:* 20.7.09), he was identifying himself with Rimbaud, whom he positively deified (See *DuS,* VI, II). David Baumgardt found that Heym knew Baudelaire and Rimbaud better than he knew any German poets, and was particularly struck by Heym's attachment to Rimbaud's 'Le bateau ivre'; but he added that Heym was no less enthusiastic about Baudelaire. According to Kurt Pinthus, Heym's poetry seemed to his poetic contemporaries to be 'eine Inkarnation Baudelaires, Poes, Rimbauds' (*DuS,* VI, 102). A number of reviewers made similar points, and Heym was generally regarded as a German Baudelaire.

With the divine Rimbaud, as he called him, Heym has much in common. Like Rimbaud he rebelled against a straightlaced upbringing; he shared the French poet's contempt for philistinism (including bourgeois morality), his vehement nature, his desire to escape altogether from European culture, and so on. His idea, in September 1911, of studying Oriental languages and becoming a dragoman, is pure Rimbaud. What was Heym's life, marked, as it was, by the same abrupt transitions of mood as Rimbaud's poetry, but a brief Season in Hell? He, no less than Rimbaud, had a *fureur de vivre;* he too sought to live with all his faculties all the time; he too was 'greedy as the sea' (Rimbaud) for the life that was to be but a dream, complaining bitterly of the monotony between the ecstasies — how often does he echo Rimbaud's words from a letter of 2 November 1870: 'Je meurs . . . dans la grisaille'. For him too the work was nothing, the act of producing it, everything. If it is true that Rimbaud's mind was 'not the mind of the artist but of the man of action', and that 'To him it was an identical act of his temperament to write the sonnet of the *vowels* and to trade in ivory and frankincense with the Arabs',[8] then this applies in a general way to Heym too, who was continually exasperated, as a poet, by the activities of his 'Wirklichkeits-mensch' *alter ego*. If it is true that Rimbaud brought into French verse something of that 'gipsy way of going with nature, as with a woman',[9] then something not so very different is true of Heym, for whom it is the *frisson*, of whatever kind, that counts. Many German poets have written more than their share of poems on death; none has written of it with greater erotic excitement. In his van Gogh essay of 1910 Carl Sternheim expressed van Gogh's relationship to reality in sexual terms, and we shall see presently that Heym idolized van Gogh; but my point here is that for Heym the aesthetic and the erotic are closely linked. Life, for him, is a matter of waiting for death (rather than God) *avec gourmandise*. No less than Rimbaud, he seeks always for the absolute and is content with nothing less. When he too feels contempt for the finished product, it is because it is by definition imperfect; the moment of consummation, whether aesthetic or erotic, is the beginning of disenchantment.

What Rimbaud gave Heym was encouragement to be himself, to ride his Fury. More specifically, to the poet he gave a visionary imagery and the starting-point for some memorable poems. There is much truth in Kurt Pinthus' comment that 'Zwar schulte Heym seine Form an der gemeisselten Strophenstrenge Baudelaires und Stefan Georges, aber wie sein französischer Vorläufer Rimbaud ballt er (zunächst) in diese unerbittliche Form nicht Gefühltes und Erlebtes, sondern: unendliche Visionen' (*DuS*, VI, 141). Thematic borrowings from Rimbaud include 'Die Tote im Wasser' (*L* 117f.) and 'Ophelia' (*L* 160ff.), both clearly indebted to 'Ophélie'. The more memorable poem is 'Die Tote im Wasser':

> Die Masten ragen an dem grauen Wall
> Wie ein verbrannter Wald ins frühe Rot,
> So schwarz wie Schlacke. Wo das Wasser tot
> Zu Speichern stiert, die morsch und im Verfall.
>
> Dumpf tönt der Schall, da wiederkehrt die Flut,
> Den Kai entlang. Der Stadtnacht Spülicht treibt
> Wie eine weiße Haut im Strom und reibt
> Sich an dem Dampfer, der im Docke ruht.
>
> Staub, Obst, Papier, in einer dicken Schicht,
> So treibt der Kot aus seinen Röhren ganz.
> Ein weißes Tanzkleid kommt, in fettem Glanz
> Ein nackter Hals und bleiweiß ein Gesicht.
>
> Die Leiche wälzt sich ganz heraus. Es bläht
> Das Kleid sich wie ein weißes Schiff im Wind.
> Die toten Augen starren groß und blind
> Zum Himmel, der voll rosa Wolken steht.

Das lila Wasser bebt von kleiner Welle.
— Der Wasserratten Fährte, die bemannen
Das weiße Schiff. Nun treibt es stolz von dannen,
Voll grauer Köpfe und voll schwarzer Felle.

Die Tote segelt froh hinaus, gerissen
Von Wind und Flut. Ihr dicker Bauch entragt
Dem Wasser groß, zerhöhlt und fast zernagt.
Wie eine Grotte dröhnt er von den Bissen.

Sie treibt ins Meer. Ihr salutiert Neptun
Von einem Wrack, da sie das Meer verschlingt,
Darinnen sie zur grünen Tiefe sinkt,
Im Arm der feisten Kraken auszuruhn.

In the last two quatrains, the girl's body, a white ship manned by water-rats
— no less memorable an image than Rimbaud's 'il a vu sur l'eau, couchée
en ses longs voiles, / La blanche Ophélie flotter, comme un grand lys' —
becomes reminiscent of the *bateau ivre;* but while the poem thus reflects the
influence on Heym of Rimbaud's poetry in general and 'Le bateau ivre' in
particular, what it really demonstrates is the power of his visual imagination and the alchemical ability, which he shares with Baudelaire, to
transmute dross into gold, horror into beauty. Other well-known poems
indebted to Rimbaud include 'Die Toten auf dem Berge' (*L* 99ff., cf. 'Bal
des pendus'), 'Der Schläfer im Walde' (*L* 40f., cf. 'Le dormeur du val'),
'Sehnsucht nach Paris' (*L* 227ff., cf. 'L'Orgie Parisienne'), 'Die Profes-
soren' (*L* 57, cf. 'Les Assis'), and 'Der Hunger' (*L* 158, cf. 'Fêtes de la faim'
and 'Les Effarés'). The list need not be extended, for what such compari-
sons show is that Rimbaud tends to spark Heym's imagination, giving him
the starting-image for a poem which then outstrips the French poet. For
instance, Rimbaud described the ecstasy of hunger in 'Les Effarés' and
personified his own hunger for life in 'Fêtes de la faim', but 'Fêtes de la faim'
is a weak affair compared with Heym's brilliantly stylized sonnet, the
imagery of which is a *tour de force:*

Er fuhr in einen Hund, dem groß er sperrt
Das rote Maul. Die blaue Zunge wirft
Sich lang heraus. Er wälzt im Staub. Er schlürft
Verwelktes Gras, das er dem Sand entzerrt.

Sein leerer Schlund ist wie ein großes Tor,
Drin Feuer sickert, langsam, tropfenweis,
Das ihm den Bauch verbrennt. Dann wäscht mit Eis
Ihm eine Hand das heiße Speiserohr.

Er wankt durch Dampf. Die Sonne ist ein Fleck,
Ein rotes Ofentor. Ein grüner Halbmond führt
Vor seinen Augen Tänze. Er ist weg.

Ein schwarzes Loch gähnt, draus die Kälte stiert,
Er fällt hinab, und fühlt noch, wie der Schreck
Mit Eisenfäusten seine Gurgel schnürt.

'Der Hunger' owes its inspiration to Rimbaud and its classical form to
Baudelaire; but what it illustrates is Heym's poetic power and originality.
Whether the *donnée* comes from life or from art — and it is normally visual —
he uses it, as here, to produce works of absolute authenticity.

If Rimbaud gave Heym much, Baudelaire gave him everything. He
identified with Baudelaire more closely than did any other poet of his
generation, although he was certainly not alone in his admiration for the
French poet. One thinks of Stefan George's appropriately elegent transla-
tion of *Les fleurs du mal,* and of the fact that *Les fleurs du mal* was an early
favourite of Georg Trakl, who, as a child, almost invariably spoke French to
his brother and sisters, a fact which helps to explain the preternatural
clarity of his work, its primitivism and naiveté. Alfred Lichtenstein's
'Gesänge an Berlin', with lines like 'O du Berlin, du bunter Stein, du Biest'
and 'Du, mein Berlin, du Opiumrausch, du Luder', clearly follow the
example of the 'Épilogue' to *Le Spleen de Paris* ('Je t'aime, ô capitale
infâme!').

Heym possessed both the immense passion and the formidable will which
Baudelaire demanded of 'extreme genius'. It was on 16 September 1911
that he noted in his diary: 'Baudelaire: Kennzeichen eines Genies: Mis-
chung aus Enthousiasmus, Sensibilität, Melancholie. Nun auf diese 3
Dinger bin ich allerdings geaicht.' On the previous day he had written
'Mein Gott — ich ersticke noch mit meinem brachliegenden Enthousiasmus in dieser banalen Zeit.' But if vehemence of feeling and imaginative
passion are basic to his work, it is the *spleen,* which he too knew all too well,
that is even more important. Hugo Ball made an admirable comparison of
Heym and Baudelaire from this point of view in 1924:

> Ich lese jetzt Georg Heym und Baudelaire gleicheitig. Es interessiert mich, weshalb sie
> so unterirdisch verzweifelt sind. Bei Baudelaire ist eine große Angst vor dem Flachen, das
> aus vier Brettern besteht und irgendwo, irgendwann einmal in die Erde verscharrt wird.
> Baudelaire klammert sich in Todesangst an die Form, an die Schönheit. Auch er könnte
> geschrieben, geschrien haben, wie Heym: 'Sterne, ich will nicht sterben!' Bei Heym ist die
> Trauer noch unheimlicher als bei dem großen Franzosen. Bei Heym ist die Trauer von der
> Sinnlosigkeit begleitet. Baudelaire glaubt an die Kunst, an die Symmetrie, an die eherne
> Form, die von den Würmern ohne Aug und Ohr nicht zernagt wird. Heym glaubt nicht
> einmal daran. Heym hat die Kunst und unerhörte Flügel, und er läßt diese Flügel
> schleifen, und die Kunst gibt ihm nur einen bitteren Nachgeschmack. Seine Verse sind
> geschrieben, als triebe er schon unterm Eise.
> Der schöne Wahnsinn! Die große, erhabene Illusion!
> In Paris kann man damit nicht ganz unglücklich werden. Aber in Deutschland?
> . . . Die Abnormitäten, die Baudelaire sammelte, sind ein Trick seiner Gestaltung. Wenn
> man seine Gedichte nacheinander liest, wirkt diese Abnormität gesucht. Baudelaire nötigt
> sich zum Verruchten, weil es da Gegensätze, schreiende Bilder, Sensationen aller fünf

Sinne gibt . . . Es ist das eine Erfindung, ein Apparat, den er sich patentieren lassen könnte. Bei Heym dagegen ist das anders. Auch er ist vom Diabolischen verführt, weil der Teufel sich mehr an die Sinne hält, als die Madonna es zu tun scheint, und ohne die Sinnlichkeit, ohne das Bunte kommt der Dichter, scheint's, nun einmal nicht aus. Heym aber hat keinen Apparat, keinen Kunstgriff. Das Leben wirkt direkt auf ihn ein. Er sieht alles so, wie er sagt. Er sieht den Abgrund, aber er sucht ihn nicht. Die Tiefe, das Stumme, verführt ihn. So ist er auch gestorben, so grauenhaft, wie seine Gedichte sind. (In: *DuS*, VI, 170)

Spleen et Idéal would make an appropriate motto for Heym's work, although *Spleen* is more in evidence than *Idéal*, which in Heym has only the connotation of Beauty and Love; his experience of *l'horreur de la vie* outweighs that of *l'extase de la vie*. Like Baudelaire, Heym 'cultivates his hysteria'; but he does not do so calmly, for his work is inspired by rage against what Dylan Thomas called the dying of the light. If Baudelaire was a moralist with, as Arthur Symons put it, a 'keen sense of the ecstasy of evil', Heym is obsessed with evil. When, as he frequently does, he writes ἀλάστωρ in his diary, he will have had both meanings of the word in mind: Fury, and he who is hounded by the Furies because he deserves to be. The only morality for him was in art. The only forms of perfection that interested him were perfect beauty and perfect love. If Baudelaire was 'le mauvais moine' of his own sonnet, an ascetic of passion, then Heym was an unashamed hedonist. That said, the beauty of his poetry — as Swinburne said of Baudelaire's — is rather passionate than sensuous; by this I mean that it is, above all, a matter of intensity. If it is true that the 'romantic' Baudelaire had something classic in his moderation, this moderation becoming at times 'as terrifying as Poe's logic' (Arthur Symons), then here is another difference, for Heym — despite the conventionality of form of much of his work, the quality which caused critics to link him with Baudelaire and, to his fury, George — was an outright enthusiast, with all the strengths and weaknesses of that ilk. He was no ascetic aesthete. He, who regarded moderation as an obscenity, was much more of a romantic than the fastidious Baudelaire. With Heym it is all or nothing; he loved Hölderlin for his very excess, although Hölderlin probably strikes us as a model of holy sobriety compared with the ferocity of his young disciple. Divine fire, passion, was what Heym lived for; nothing else mattered to him. In what is, I think, one of his greatest poems, the sonnet 'Der Hunger', he has given classical expression to the hunger for life of the being bearing death's mark on its brow — for who can doubt that Heym's dog stands for the poet himself, who heard too soon what his revered Keats called 'The thunder of the trumpets of the night'?

There are other facts, too, which are no less relevant to Heym's sense of kinship with Baudelaire, among them the pervading sense of spiritual tragedy in both men's work, the thirst for glory and diabolical thirst for fame which Heym shared with the French poet, his passionate devotion to passion, his preoccupation with suffering, his craving for beauty, his love of art (especially painting), his sense of being misunderstood, and, above all, his saturnine temperament and obsession with evil: 'alles was geschieht, ist und wird böse' (*T:* 26.6.10). What Joanna Richardson has said of Baudelaire — 'Baudelaire shows a Romantic — indeed a Gothic — concern with death and corruption, a Romantic interest in violence, a Romantic nostalgia for the past, a Romantic longing for escape to eternity or to exotic climes'[10] — is entirely applicable to Heym, whose enthusiasm for Baudelaire's poetry can be explained in several ways. The Berlin poems of Heym and Lichtenstein (and of many of their less gifted contemporaries) belong together not so much with the Berlin poems of earlier German poets (Julius Hart; Richard Dehmel, whose vitalism Heym admired), as with Baudelaire's poems about Paris and Rimbaud's poems about London. Heym's 'Berlin' sonnet-cycle could equally well have been called 'Le Spleen de Berlin'. As urban poets, Heym, Hoddis and Lichtenstein are all indebted to the imagery of Baudelaire's *cité fourmillante,* for Baudelaire,

> gave new possibilities to poetry in a new stock of imagery of contemporary life . . . It is not merely in the use of imagery of common life, not merely in the use of imagery of the sordid life of a great metropolis, but in the elevation of such imagery to the *first intensity* — presenting it as it is, and yet making it represent something much more than itself — that Baudelaire has created a mode of release and expression for other men.[11]

This seems to me to apply exactly to Georg Heym, who is, among other things, an urban poet in precisely this sense of simultaneously seeing the megapolis of Berlin realistically *and* symbolically. But not only is much of Heym's imagery a demonized urban imagery; he also shares with Baudelaire a sense of the unreality of this and any other reality. In his diary he quotes Baudelaire with evident approval: 'Der gesunde Verstand sagt uns, daß die Dinge der Erde nur sehr wenige Realität besitzen, und daß es wahre Wirklichkeit nur in den Träumen giebt. Baudelaire' (*T:* 15.9.11). The form of much of his most characteristic work is a reflection of Baudelaire's form, and a few of his poems echo poems by Baudelaire; thus 'Der Tod der Liebenden' (*L* 151–4) was inspired by 'La mort des amants'.

Because there was no way out of it, save into death, around which all his deepest fears were clustered, he saw life with Baudelaire as 'Le monde, monotone . . . un désert d'ennui!' The monotone of so much of his poetry is the clearest expression of the monotony of life, which he experienced as a wasteland, a vicious circle, a prison, an Inferno. It makes little difference whether a poem is entitled 'Die Menschen' (*L* 431f.: 'Die Menschen gehen schattenhaft im Kreise, / In leerer Wege ausgetretnem Gleise') or 'Die Gefangenen I' (*L* 122: 'Sie trampeln um den Hof im engen Kreis'), for the circle is equally vicious; the prison, like Schopenhauer's penitentiary and Kafka's penal colony, is that of life. Of life, that is, as experienced by Heym himself. A diary entry dated 28 May 1911 — 'Mein Gehirn rennt

immer im Kreise herum wie ein Gefangener, der an die Kerkertür haut' —
shows that, for all its visual starting–point in a painting by van Gogh, 'Die
Gefangenen, I' is a highly personal poem. Here it is:

> Sie trampeln um den Hof im engen Kreis.
> Ihr Blick schweift hin und her im kahlen Raum.
> Er sucht nach einem Feld, nach einem Baum,
> Und prallt zurück von kahler Mauern Weiß.
>
> Wie in den Mühlen dreht der Rädergang,
> So dreht sich ihrer Schritte schwarze Spur.
> Und wie ein Schädel mit der Mönchstonsur,
> So liegt des Hofes Mitte kahl und blank.
>
> Es regnet dünn auf ihren kurzen Rock.
> Sie schaun betrübt die graue Wand empor,
> Wo kleine Fenster sind, mit Kasten vor,
> Wie schwarze Waben in dem Bienenstock.
>
> Man treibt sie ein, wie Schafe zu der Schur.
> Die grauen Rücken drängen in den Stall.
> Und klappernd schallt heraus der Widerhall
> Der Holzpantoffeln auf dem Treppenflur.

Heym's work is furious, ferocious, feral even, because he felt like a
trapped animal, imprisoned in time; knowing intuitively that he had no
future, he was unable to escape from the *cercle vicieux* of his own *angoisse*, his
ennui, his *spleen* (he was himself liable to slip into the language of his most
revered models). This is why he writes in 'Mit den fahrenden Schiffen' (*L*
457f.) that 'Alles war schon vorzeiten. Und kehret wieder sich um'. There is
no way; there is no escape. The way obsesses him as much as it does Kafka:
'Ich weiß nicht mehr, wo mein Weg hingeht . . . Jetzt ist alles dunkel,
auseinander, zerstreut', he wrote in his diary on 9 October 1911, and at
about the same time the same feeling reappears in the poem 'Mitte des
Winters' (*L* 438):

> Weglos ist jedes Leben. Und verworren
> Ein jeder Pfad. Und keiner weiß das Ende,
> Und wer da suchet, daß er Einen fände,
> Der sieht ihn stumm, und schüttelnd leere Hände.

It was two months after this that he referred to himself as 'Georg Heym. Der
nicht den Weg weiß.' What he meant was that he knew there was for him no
way to meaning, or fulfilment, or life. He was indeed the brother of·
Baudelaire, although this must not blind us to the differences between the
two poets, particularly the fact that whereas *Les fleurs du mal* is the work of a
Christian poet, *Der ewige Tag* is not.

Visions of Hell

'Why, this is Hell, nor can [*sic*] I out of it!' Arthur Symons imagined Baudelaire voicing to himself these words of Marlowe's Mephistopheles.[12] It is equally easy to imagine Heym voicing them, for he too, no less than the great 19th-century pessimists, viewed life as Hell. Indeed, Marlowe — one of the writers Heym most revered — gave in his *Doctor Faustus* a definition of Hell that corresponds with Heym's:

Faust:	Tell me, where is the place that men call hell?
Mephistopheles:	Within the bowels of these elements,
	Where we are tortur'd and remain for ever:
	Hell hath no limits, nor is circumscrib'd
	In one self place; for where we are is hell,
	And where hell is, there must we ever be . . .

In charting what he sees as Hell on earth, Heym writes with a cold chagrin reminiscent of *Les Litanies de Satan* and of *Spleen et Idéal*; his 'Ich verfluche dich Gott' (*L* 18) parallels Baudelaire's 'mon semblable, ô mon maître, je te maudis' ('Le Voyage, 6'), except that his agony is without any Christian solace. His 'Die Hölle I' (*L* 327f.) depicts a Dantesque Inferno in that Heym too 'took the raw material of his Hell from this world and yet made a very proper Hell of it' (Schopenhauer on Dante, in *Die Welt als Wille und Vorstellung*, Book IV). He can envisage nothing more Hellish than the ennui which he experienced and which Schopenhauer charted:

Ich dachte viel der Schrecken zu erfahren,
Als ich an ihren hohen Toren stand,
Abgründe rot und Meere voller Brand
Hinter den großen Riegeln zu gewahren,

Und sah ein Land voll ausgespannter Öde,
Und Monde bleich, wie ein paar starre Tränen.
Man gab mir keinen Gruß zurück. Nur blöde
Sahn mich die Schatten an mit lautem Gähnen.

Die Unterwelt, sie gleicht zu sehr der Erde:
Im Schlamm des Hades lag ein Krokodil.
Man warf auch hier nach seinem Kopf zum Spiel,
Vielleicht mit etwas müderer Gebärde.

Wanderer gingen in den Sonntagsröcken,
Sie sprachen von den Sorgen dieser Wochen
Und freuten sich, wenn junge Falten krochen
Aus ihrer Freunde Stirn wie Dornenhecken.

Laternen wurden durch die Nacht geschwungen,
Und einen Toten trug man uns vorbei.

Er war im ewig grauen Einerlei
Vor Langeweile wie ein Pilz zersprungen.

It was at about this time that Heym wrote 'Mir hat der Satan die Kunst des Malens versagt.' He went on: 'Und was würde ich malen? . . . Die Toten im Wolkenberge. Vorn die Pfeifer. Oben in dem einsamen höllischen Licht.' (*T:* July/August 1911). Hell, for him, is not only death; it is the solitude of life. The recurrent imagery of his poetry speaks for itself:

Endloser Zug, wie eine schwarze Mauer,
Die durch die Himmel läuft, durch Wüstenei
Der winterlichen Städte in der Trauer
Verschneiter Himmel, und dem Einerlei

Der Riesenflächen, die sich fern verlieren
In endlos weißes Weiß am fernen Saum.
('Die Wanderer': *L* 190f.)

On reading these lines one thinks not only of Baudelaire, but also of Nietzsche, whose poem 'Vereinamt' prefigures Heym's imagery: 'Die Welt — ein Tor / zu tausend Wüsten stumm und kalt!' It was Nietzsche who saw man as the wanderer 'zur Winter-Wanderschaft verflucht', and who wrote: 'Kein Pfad mehr! Abgrund rings und Totenstille!' And one thinks, too, of Kafka's K standing alone in the snow, seeking in vain for the way that does not lead into death. But these close parallels must not distract us from the fact that it is his own deepest and most insistent experience that Heym is describing here. That said, when he writes in his diary that 'Nichts steht dem Menschen mehr an, als Leid und Weinen. Und dazwischen die Langeweile, Langeweile'(*T:* 27.12.09), this could be Schopenhauer describing the burden of existence.

If Baudelaire is Heym's poet, his philosopher is Schopenhauer. His interest in Schopenhauer dates back to summer 1905, when we find him pondering suicide: 'Ich habe Furcht vor dem Leben. Zwar gibt es Stunden, da ich mich unermeßlich glücklich fühlte, aber mit wieviel Schmerzen habe ich's erkauft. Sanftes Nirwana, Aufgehen in das All. Zwar sage ich mir ja auch,"Unser Leben ist eine Torheit, die andere begangen habeñ, aber ich wünsche trotz allem, trotz allem doch zu leben' (*T:* 4 June 1905). The determinedly pessimistic frame of mind in which he had gone to Neuruppin had got out of hand, had turned into the 'qualvolle[r] unfruchtbare[r] Pessimismus' which was to dog him for the rest of his life. How much of Schopenhauer he had read in 1905, is not clear; what is certain is that he read 'Über den Tod' in 1906, probably in a selection which included 'Das Leben der Gattung,' 'Die Erblichkeit der Eigenschaften,' and, possibly, 'Zur Metaphysik der Geschlechtsliebe'. In 1910 he borrowed the whole of Schopenhauer from David Baumgardt; when it was eventually returned, two blank pages of *Die Welt als Wille und Vorstellung* were adorned with a typical 'Heymerei'. We may safely assume that he read the famous Fourth Book of *Die Welt als Wille und Vorstellung*, which contains much that parallels his own view of life (life as Hell on earth; the prison of life; ennui; the vanity and suffering of life; death; the suicide theme; etc.). Just as some of Heym's most characteristic images are paralleled in van Gogh, so too a number of his typical ideas are foreshadowed in Schopenhauer. His Hell, both in 'Die Hölle, I' and in 'Die Vorstadt' (*L:* 133f) is that described by Schopenhauer ('Die Welt ist eben die Hölle'); as such it reminds one of Mad Jack's vision in George Gissing's novel *The Nether World* ('You are passing through a state of punishment . . . This life you are now leading is that of the damned; this place to which you are confined is Hell! There is no escape for you . . . This is Hell — Hell — Hell!'). This Hell is characterized by what Heym (like Baudelaire) found to be, and what Schopenhauer described as, one of the main features of life: ennui. But Heym was not, of course, a Schopenhauerian; he was not even a thinker, as his reported reaction to the mention of Kant ('Jotte doch, die verdammte transzendente Logik') shows. His 'philosophy' was existential, visceral, beyond his control. He must have admired Schopenhauer, above all, as an artist in words, someone who said exactly what he thought both forcefully and with style. He will have been attracted by Schopenhauer's lucubrations on the subject of death, and will, of course, have approved Schopenhauer's view of Art as man's momentary deliverance from the toils of life, but I doubt that Heym, had he lived, would have come round to sharing the philosopher's view of the wisdom of renunciation; it is much more likely that he, like Verlaine, would have refused to learn from experience, would have scorned to subjugate his will–to–life, would have remained passionately in love with life until whatever other quietus it prepared for him.

Among Heym's best-known and most characteristic poems are those in which he conveys his view of the modern *cité maudite* as possessed by demons, that is, by uncontrollable forces which destroy man from within; in a review of his friend's work, Ernst Balcke said that it was the 'dämonische Maßlosigkeit' of Berlin that obsessed Heym; he added 'Und so symbolisiert sich die Stadt in einem riesenhaften Baal, und in der Gestalt unheilvoll wirkender "Dämonen".' (*Die Aktion*, 8 May 1911, repr. in *DuS*, VI, 194). Balcke is referring to 'Der Gott der Stadt' (*L* 192) and 'Die Dämonen der Städte' (*L* 186f.); his comment is useful but also shows that he did not — as Heym knew — fully understand his friend's work. The better of these two poems is 'Der Gott der Stadt', written in December 1910, which appeared in *Der ewige Tag* (ironically named because the only eternal thing in Heym's city of the damned is the damnation itself). Heym's omnipresent demons represent, ultimately, the curse of existence. There are cognate figures in Indian and Tibetan demonology, and a related philosophy is far closer at hand, in the work of Schopenhauer. With Heym's demons brooding over the cities whose evil they personify it is also interesting to compare a series of drawings in *Simplicissimus*, which Heym is known to have read. K.L. Schneider has drawn attention to two drawings by Heinrich Kley which appeared in *Simplicissimus* on 20 July and 16 August 1909 and reappeared in Kley's *Skizzenbuch* (1909); they are reproduced in Schneider's *Zerbrochene Formen*.[13] There is also a drawing by Max Slevogt which appeared in *Simplicissimus* in 1896; this drawing, reproduced by Soergel,[14] offers an even closer parallel to 'Der Gott der Stadt' and 'Der Krieg' than do Kley's drawings. All three drawings depict a gigantic devil standing over a chaotic scene. There is, finally, Goya's 'A Giant' of 1808-10, which depicts a crowd fleeing from its fears, these being represented by a striding giant; Heym admired Goya's work. Here is Heym's verbal image:

Auf einem Häuserblocke sitzt er breit.
Die Winde lagern schwarz um seine Stirn.
Er schaut voll Wut, wo fern in Einsamkeit
Die letzten Häuser in das Land verirrn.

Vom Abend glänzt der rote Bauch dem Baal,
Die großen Städte knien um ihn her.
Der Kirchenglocken ungeheure Zahl
Wogt auf zu ihm aus schwarzer Türme Meer.

Wie Korybanten-Tanz dröhnt die Musik
Der Millionen durch die Straßen laut.
Der Schlote Rauch, die Wolken der Fabrik
Ziehn auf zu ihm, wie Duft von Weihrauch blaut.

Das Wetter schwelt in seinen Augenbrauen.
Der dunkle Abend wird in Nacht betäubt.
Die Stürme flattern, die wie Geier schauen
Von seinem Haupthaar, das im Zorne sträubt.

Er streckt ins Dunkel seine Fleischerfaust.
Er schüttelt sie. Ein Meer von Feuer jagt
Durch eine Straße. Und der Glutqualm braust
Und frißt sie auf, bis spät der Morgen tagt.

'Der Gott der Stadt' is written in iambic pentameters in 4-line blocks with alternating rhymes which stop after five stanzas, but which could equally well have gone on indefinitely ('Die Dämonen der Städte' has twelve stanzas and its relative weakness has nothing to do with length). The iambics are as forceful as the trochaics of the somewhat later 'Der Krieg' (discussed below), and there are other features which link the poems. There War is personified as a demon crushing the moon in his black hand; here the winds swirling around Baal's brow are black, black as the destruction which he brings. The wind is animated and demonized by Heym's characteristic use of the plural. And yet this Baal, whose naming is delayed — a trick which Heym learnt from Hölderlin — until the second stanza, seems at this stage like nothing more than a *persona* of Georg Heym himself looking out, 'voll Wut', over Charlottenburg to where the last houses of the demonically expanding megapolis (the population of Charlottenburg rose from 20,000 in 1871 to 323,000 in 1919!) are lost in a hostile environment. Besides, Baal's Roman equivalent is Bacchus, and 'Bacchus' was one of Heym's nicknames among his *Saufbrüder*. This 'Gott der Stadt' is therefore, among other things, the 21-year old poet wishing death and destruction upon the philistine metropolis by which he was fascinated.

Baal's belly gleaming red in the evening sun represents his appetite for death and Heym's appetite for life; that the monstrous noise of the church bells rises from a sea of *black* towers suggests that Heym sees Christianity as life-denying. And so on. The poem contains a number of images which confirm that what Heym is describing here is both the real Berlin-Charlottenburg and, simultaneously, a symbolical monster city of the imagination. Baal is both a symbol of the deathly forces of modern life, and a personification of Heym as rebel.

The tension between the explosive violence of Heym's imagery and his wooden verse forms produces the dance of death effect noted by Ernst Stadler in his review of *Der ewige Tag* in *Cahiers Alsaciens* in May 1912; there is also a high degree of alienation involved, for the explosive force of the imagery both mocks the form and is itself ridiculed by it. Many of Heym's poems show not only this tension between conventional verse-form and a markedly unconventional imagery, but also a fundamental discord between his horrified visions and the sobriety with which they are described. There is a similar discord in Lichtenstein's work. In Heym's case at least the nonchalance is a mask. Stadler was the first to comment on what is a basic feature of Heym's mature poetic work: 'eine gewisse Inkongruenz zwischen der formalen Starrheit und der ungestüm über die metrischen Schranken hinausdrängenden Bildkraft.' The central section of Stadler's review remains to this day the best single account of Heym's basic poetic technique:

Freilich findet sich bei Heym nichts von dem stürmischen Überschwang, mit dem etwa Verhaeren die Größe unserer Zeit und die Wunder der großen Städte gefeiert hat. Heyms ernstes und festes Jasagen ist einem Gefühl abgerungen, das ganz mit den Drohungen und Schrecknissen des Lebens angefüllt ist. Wenn er die Großstadt malt, gibt er Bilder der Elenden, Siechen und Bettler, zeigt er die Spitäler, in deren Gängen die Krankheiten gespenstisch wie Marionetten umhersteigen, die Höhlen des Elends, den Schmutz und Hunger der Vorstadtgassen, wo zerlumpte Greise an Sommerabenden reglos vor engen Türen kauern, und der Lärm aus den Stuben dringt, in denen verwahrloste Kinder mit welken Eltern zusammengepfercht sind. Heym ist ein Priester der Schrecken. Ein Visionär des Grauenerregenden und Grotesken. Ein Bruder der Poe und Baudelaire (diesem verwandt auch in der Strenge seiner Rhythmik und der metrischen Gefüge), und mehr noch vielleicht der Rops und Kubin. Ganz hingenommen im Anschaun seiner Gesichte, gleichsam erstarrt von ihrer Furchtbarkeit, aber ohne fühlbares Mitschwingen der Seele, ohne lyrische Bewegtheit, ganz der gegenständlichen Gewalt seiner Bilder anheimgegeben, deren oft ins Grelle und Ungeheuerliche verzerrte Umrisse er mit wuchtigen, harten, kühlen Strichen nachzeichnet. Die strenge Sachlichkeit, die unerschütterlich Bild an Bild reiht, ohne jemals abzuirren, ins Unbestimmte auszuschweifen; die starre Regelmäßigkeit seiner Rhythmik, die ein gärendes, brausendes Chaos in eine knappe und gleichsam unbewegte Form sperrt, geben mit der Fremdartigkeit seiner Vorwürfe die seltsamste Wirkung: ein Totentanz in den verbindlichen Formen höfischen Zeremoniells. Gedichte wie 'Louis Capet', 'Robespierre', 'Ophelia' sind von einer hohen Vollkommenheit. Bei anderen fühlt man störend eine gewisse Inkongruenz zwischen der formalen Starrheit und der ungestüm über die metrischen Schranken hinausdrängenden Bildkraft. Wäre es Heym vergönnt gewesen, sein starkes Talent auszureifen, so hätte er wohl noch seine Form, seinen persönlichen Rhythmus gefunden.

Knowing Heym's early and as then unpublished poems, to say nothing of *Umbra vitae*, we (unlike Stadler in 1912) are in a position to say that *Der ewige Tag* is a unified collection of Heym's *most powerful* poems at that time, but one which does no sort of justice to the tonal range of which he was capable.

An excellent illustration of Stadler's basic criticism, and of much else besides, is Heym's best-known poem, 'Der Krieg' (*L* 346f.):

Aufgestanden ist er, welcher lange schlief,
Aufgestanden unten aus Gewölben tief.
In der Dämmerung steht er, groß und unerkannt,
Und den Mond zerdrückt er in der schwarzen Hand.

In den Abendlärm der Städte fällt es weit,
Frost und Schatten einer fremden Dunkelheit,
Und der Märkte runder Wirbel stockt zu Eis.
Es wird still. Sie sehn sich um. Und keiner weiß.

In den Gassen faßt es ihre Schulter leicht.
Eine Frage. Keine Antwort. Ein Gesicht erbleicht.
In der Ferne wimmert ein Geläute dünn
Und die Bärte zittern um ihr spitzes Kinn.

Auf den Bergen hebt er schon zu tanzen an
Und er schreit: Ihr Krieger alle, auf und an.
Und es schallet, wenn das schwarze Haupt er schwenkt,
Drum von tausend Schädeln laute Kette hängt.

Einem Turm gleich tritt er aus die letzte Glut,
Wo der Tag flieht, sind die Ströme schon voll Blut.
Zahllos sind die Leichen schon im Schilf gestreckt,
Von des Todes starken Vögeln weiß bedeckt.

In die Nacht er jagt das Feuer querfeldein
Einen roten Hund mit wilder Mäuler Schrein.
Aus dem Dunkel springt der Nächte schwarze Welt,
Von Vulkanen furchtbar ist ihr Rand erhellt.

Und mit tausend roten Zipfelmützen weit
Sind die finstren Ebnen flackend überstreut,
Und was unten auf den Straßen wimmelnd flieht,
Stößt er in die Feuerwälder, wo die Flamme brausend zieht.

Und die Flammen fressen brennend Wald um Wald,
Gelbe Fledermäuse zackig in das Laub gekrallt.
Seine Stange haut er wie ein Köhlerknecht
In die Bäume, daß das Feuer brause recht.

Eine große Stadt versank in gelbem Rauch,
Warf sich lautlos in des Abgrunds Bauch.
Aber riesig über glühnden Trümmern steht
Der in wilde Himmel dreimal seine Fackel dreht,

Über sturmzerfetzter Wolken Widerschein,
In des toten Dunkels kalte Wüstenein,
Daß er mit dem Brande weit die Nacht verdorr,
Pech und Feuer träufet unten auf Gomorrh.

Heym was obsessed by a foreboding of war and, at the same time, longed for it as a forceful interruption of the monotony of his young life and of the banality of the age. In his diary he wrote: 'Auch ich kann sagen: Gäb es nur Krieg, gesund wär' ich. Ein Tag ist wie der andere. Keine großen Freuden, keine großen Schmerzen' (T: 30.5.07). After a number of similar entries he adds, on 15 September 1911: 'ich ersticke noch mit meinem brachliegenden Enthousiasmus in der banalen Zeit.' Such was his longing for an heroic life — the most that man can hope for, according to Schopenhauer — that he even dreamt, in 1911, of taking part in great battles. The disparity between his dream of glory and his vision, in this poem, of the carnage to which the heroic leads, is striking. The form of the poem carries clear intimations of the heroic mode, but none whatsoever of the expected immortality. The pervasive enthusiasm is without any illusions; the 'heroic' line is wooden, so that the poem is more like a dance of death than anything else. When Heym wrote it in early September 1911, 'Der Krieg' must have been a visualization of that great battle of which he dreamt; when it was read by others, however, it seemed a prophetic vision of the Great War for Civilization.

What strikes the reader at once is the monumental impersonality and barbaric grandeur of the poem, which differs from most 1914-18 war-poems in being not at all subjective. What Heym gives is an objective picture of war as such, war as an elemental feature of life; there is terror in this objectivity. His poem aims to shock; it consists of juxtaposed explosive images which burst like shells in the reader's mind, a technique that was to be further developed in 1914/15, in poetry of a very different kind, by August Stramm. Since the poet sees war as an elemental feature of life, 'Der Krieg' ultimately conveys a visionary and prophetic picture of reality itself.

The heavy six-beat trochaic line in which the poem is written makes the accent stalk through the poem like the incarnate demon of war through his apocalyptic landscape. The rhythm and imagery of the poem underline the extreme violence of its subject matter. Occasional deviations from the metrical pattern give the impression both of the poet's vision dominating and threatening to violate his formal resources, and of violence continually erupting through the surface of life; the old world represented by the trochaic metre is continually burst open by the violence of the anarchic subject matter. The use of rhymed couplets throughout, with all the rhymes masculine ones, is highly appropriate since the rhyme scheme thus reflects and expresses the primitive, elemental quality of Heym's subject. The poem is lyrical above all in its Keatsian concentration.

The opening of 'Der Krieg' is majestic in its barbaric grandeur. War is immediately personified into an infernal demon who rises from below, from the collective unconscious, from the primitive depths of life, and at the end stands in all his grim majesty over the apocalyptic landscape that is both his own true element and the scene of mankind's Fall and Passion. What, if not War, is 'die große Gewalt, die uns unbewußt erscheint' of which Heym wrote in his diary in October 1911? The demon War rises before our eyes on the repeated word 'aufgestanden'. One changed syllable — 'auferstanden' — and the word would refer to a god rising from the dead. But 'aufgestanden' is appropriate here, for War is a chthonic god or demon, a great and unknown power, a figure of utter profanity. Just how terrible this power is, is suggested in the last line of the first stanza, where War is shown crushing the moon in his brute black hand; his colour is the colour of evil and death, for war is the product of evil, and the product of war, its whole point and purpose, is death. The demon War whose name is Death brings with him the chill of life-denying darkness. In his awful presence life in the city of man is paralysed. At first people are nonplussed; but then the uncanny, threatening atmosphere gets to them and puzzlement gives way to fear. The jerky, abrupt phrases punch home the confused reactions of men jerked out of their trivial routines who suddenly find themselves faced with the primeval violence which all the time had been lurking at the bottom of their own minds (*homo homini lupus*). The peal of bells is a *memento mori* which reduces the staid bourgeois to a figure of fun.

The scene now changes; from the city terrified by this sudden eruption of hitherto suppressed violence we see the demon War moving out into the landscape of war, a landscape that becomes increasingly a prophetic picture of what has been called 'the lunar waste of the Somme', until it finally assumes the proportions of myth, of something wholly uncontrollable. Personification is repeatedly used to add to the terror. Thus in the sixth stanza night, the abode of demons, is touched into independent existence by Heym's use of the plural 'nights', which implies a black world full of night-demons. Similarly fire is animated into 'a red hound with the screaming of wild mouths': the mythical hell-hound itself carrying off the broken animal bodies of the dead, across the once-green fields, to eternal damnation. One thinks of van Gogh trying to express the terrible passions of humanity by means of red and green. The volcanoes which light up the edge of the night-demons' world fill the air with the sulphurous stench of damnation, pointing forward to the final Apocalypse.

In the seventh stanza Death is again personified, this time as a monstrous stoker feeding the flames with the countless dead in their tall pointed caps (the 'Pickelhauben' of the German war-dead in 1914). The whole world is turned into a ghastly crematorium. In a brilliant nightmare-image which derives from van Gogh, the flames are described as 'Gelbe Fledermäuse zackig in das Laub gekrallt'; the purpose of this memorable metaphor is to be nightmarish; in one of his prose sketches Heym identifies the bat as 'die Fledermaus des Todes', an image which may have been suggested by the white bats of the Potsdamer Platz (which feature in Paul Boldt's poem 'Auf der Terrasse des Café Josty') or even by the 'Fledermauszimmer' of the Nollendorf-Casino, in which the poets of the Neuer Club used to meet. And still the strutting, mechanical rhythms go their incessant, senseless way.

All through the poem War is presented as the sign of evil, and at the end we see the original monster city destroyed by War, destroyed, that is, by the awakened evil within itself. Its fall is made to echo the Fall of Babylon the Great, but as the earth is reduced to a wasteland dominated by the gigantic figure of Death Triumphant, Christian iconography fails, for Death is, finally, reminiscent of the Hindu destroyer-god Siva Bhairava with his garland of a thousand skulls, and similar figures from Tibetan demonology. Heym's source for this image may well be Schopenhauer's *Die Welt als Wille und Vorstellung*, which he read in 1910 and which contains, in the famous Fourth Book, a reference to 'Schiwa . . . mit dem Halsband von Todten-köpfen.'

The Painter *Manqué*

As we have seen, Heym's imagination was primarily visual. If Baudelaire's work has what Swinburne called 'a quality of drawing', then Heym's poems have a quality of painting. Erwin Loewenson reported that Heym 'dachte überhaupt nur in Optisch-Konkretem' (*DuS*, VI, 46). He was as much an *Augenmensch* as Kafka. He saw everything in images, these immediately taking on a symbolical dimension in his mind. His poems are brilliantly, vividly visual: they can always be seen and could easily be painted. They are the work of a man with a painter's eye. His black visions have, often, an appalling clarity — one thinks of the nightmare vision of a group of demons standing round the woman giving birth to a headless child. Such images burn themselves into the memory. Heym was in fact a painter *manqué*; even in this he resembles Baudelaire. In July/August 1911 we find him recording in his diary: 'Mir hat der Satan die Kunst des Malens versagt.' He proceeds to describe in detail four paintings that he would paint if he were able to do so, and cries out in exasperation: 'Warum hat mir der Himmel die Gabe der Zeichnung versagt. Imaginationen peinigen mich, wie nie einen Maler vor mir'. It is these 'Imaginationen' that fill his poems. Possibly the last lines that he ever wrote:

Licht. Taghell. Blutrot.
Musik. Weiße Clowns
Die Königsärge schwanken auf den Schultern.
Strohköpfe auf langen Besen.
Waffenröcke
Der ganze . . .
(*L* 515)

read like notes not so much for a poem, as for a painting. He would also have liked to be a sculptor. His diary contains these entries, just one week apart: 'Ich möchte ein Bildhauer sein, dann würde ich die Liebe darstellen. Ein Jüngling, der dasteht, als hätte man ihm in die Stirn gehauen, wie ein Narr, wie ein Verwundeter' (*T:* 21.8.08), 'oder die Schlacht bei Marathon malen. Eine sandige Ebene. Und von der Sonne beglänzt zieht die Reihe der Griechen in das Tal' (*T:* 28.8.08). For a poet of Heym's power, this is an extraordinary state of affairs, especially when one remembers that his 'Marathon' cycle includes more images than any painting (except by Bosch) ever could. Unlike some of his contemporaries, Heym does not blame the language for his own inability to find the right words; but he does make it abundantly clear that he would not write if he could paint.

It is hardly surprising that one of Heym's major enthusiasms was the work of van Gogh. His interest in van Gogh dates from 1909/10. On 2 September 1910 he wrote to John Wolfsohn that van Gogh 'sieht alle Farben so, wie ich sie sehe. Ich habe beim Lesen mir so und so oft gesagt: Donnerwetter, genau so würdest Du ein Gedicht machen: Die Matrosen vor der Sonnenscheibe. Die lila Kähne. Der Sämann in einem unendlichen Feld, etc. Nur: daß Malen sehr schwer ist. Und Dichten so unendlich leicht, wenn man nur Optik hat' (*DuS*, III, 205). In a memoir of Heym (see *DuS*, VI, 144), John Wolfsohn wrote that this letter was written 'unter dem erschütternden Eindruck einer Ausstellung van Goghscher Bilder und der Lektüre van Goghscher Briefe.' This means that the book which Heym borrowed from John Wolfsohn was van Gogh's *Briefe* (ed. Margarete Mauthner, 1906), and also implies that he attended the 19th Secession (November 1909 — January 1910) at which 19 works by van Gogh were shown; presumably he also subsequently attended the large van Gogh exhibition held at the Kunstsalon Paul Cassirer from 25 October to 20 November 1910.

No doubt many factors combined to make the experience of seeing a number of works by van Gogh and reading his letters so 'shattering' for Heym. The fact that he shared van Gogh's keen eye for colour and for the *Dinglichkeit der Welt* was a major factor, but even more important, I think, will have been the fact that he perceived and found in van Gogh a kindred genius with similar urges, obsessions and fears, for 'What distinguishes his [van Gogh's] entire oeuvre is its excess, excessive power, excessive nervousness, violence and expressiveness . . . He is one of the exalted, an enemy of bourgeois sobriety and meticulous accuracy, a sort of drunken giant'.[15] This could be a description of Heym, whose work has the same kind of dramatic intensity and expressive pathos as the Dutchman's. John Wolfsohn could not have chosen a stronger word to describe the impact of van Gogh's work and letters on Heym; the word 'erschüttert' implies that Heym was profoundly shaken, 'shattered' to the point of being upset. Even given Heym's volatile, mercurial temperament, such a reaction is only explicable if what he has seen has led him to identify with van Gogh. I have shown elsewhere that this was the case.[16] Heym was, like van Gogh, an outsider, a loner uncertain of his own identity. There is a revealing parallel between van Gogh's self-portraits and Heym's — relatively fewer — poems about himself, which are no less astonishingly objective and yet no less narcissistic. Presumably their difficulties in defining themselves were one of the factors which made both men melancholy to the point of being suicidal. Heym's poems are as much a cry of anguish as van Gogh's paintings; but he lacks van Gogh's saintly humility. For Heym, even more than for other writers of his generation, van Gogh will have been what he himself became: tragic man. The Expressionist generation was fascinated not only by van Gogh's use of expressive colour and expressive line, but by his exemplary heroism and tragedy. Above all, however, van Gogh meant 'having the courage to express oneself'.[17]

Heym will, then, have found in van Gogh many of his own human problems and artistic solutions. If the power of van Gogh's *daimon* will have been frightening, the example of van Gogh's expressionism — for that is what it is — must have encouraged him to go on with what he had already begun. As he does so, he includes a number of clearly recognizable van Gogh motifs in his work. It may be that some of the echoes of van Gogh in his work from January 1910 to October 1911 are tributes to one further along his own road; at all events, they show that Heym recognized a kindred spirit and a great artist when he saw him.

Paintings by van Gogh gave Heym the starting-point for some of his poems. Thus 'Die Gefangenen, I' (*L* 122), for instance, was prompted by

'La ronde des prisonniers' ('Prisoners' Round' or 'The Prison Court-Yard'), which was itself transcribed into oil from a drawing, 'Newgate — The Exercise Yard', in Gustav Doré's *London, A Pilgrimage* (1872); Heym's first stanza is a verbalization, somewhat in the style of Rilke's *Neue Gedichte*, of van Gogh's image. In both cases the prisoners are the victims of a life represented by the bare walls. The poem 'Die drei Bäume' (*L* 107) of August 1910 may have been prompted by van Gogh's 'Three Trees and a House', and a number of van Gogh's favourite motifs reappear in other poems: the sower (cf. Heym's reference to 'Der Sämann in einem unendlichen Feld': *DuS*, III, 205) or man ploughing is seen in poems like 'Printemps' (*L* 261: 'Ein Ackerer geht groß am Himmelsrand'), the 'bearers of the burden' or miners' women carrying sacks appear in 'Die Menschen' (*L* 431f.: 'Die Menschen gehen . . . / Stumm mit den Säcken gegen den Himmelsrand'), and the row of flame-like cypresses can be seen in 'Die Heimat der Toten, II' (*L* 208-11: 'Ein Totenhain, und Lorbeer, Baum an Baum, / Wie grüne Flammen, die der Wind bewegt'). 'Die Irren im Garten' (*L* 418) may be indebted to van Gogh's related paintings and sketches, but need not be, for Heym (like Hoddis and Lichtenstein) was fascinated by the mental hospitals of Berlin-West. But van Gogh's memorable bat-painting, 'Stuffed Kalong', must surely have been in Heym's mind when he used the image of the yellow bat-flames in 'Der Krieg, I', for van Gogh's bat is vividly flame-coloured; it is already fire personified. There are many other parallels. The long and the short of it is, however, that Heym was himself a painter *manqué*. This is shown by a diary-entry in which he wrote: 'Ich habe jetzt für Farben einen geradezu wahnsinnigen Sinn. Ich sehe ein Beet mit einer Menge roter Stauden und darüber einen tiefblauen kühlen Herbsthimmel und fühle mich maaslos entzückt' (*T:* 25.9.10). Poetic evidence for this obsession with colour can be found throughout his work; a case in point is the poem 'Blau. Weiß. Grün' (*L* 62), written in April 1910; others dating from about the same time, are 'April' (*L* 66) and 'Autumnus' (*L* 129). The colours in question in 'Blau. Weiß. Grün' may have been suggested by something as trivial as the colours of the Tennisklub Blau-Weiß and/or of the Corps Rhenania; but what remains is a scene in which, as in van Gogh's letters, words are used as substitutes for the colours which they denote.

Like Baudelaire, Heym was fascinated by clouds. In each case it was probably to the artist within that they appealed so strongly. On 29 June 1910 he wrote in his diary that 'Man sollte nichts tun, als immer den Wolken zuschauen, den weiten geheimnisvollen Wolken', and in the poem 'O Wolkenland . . . '(*L* 699f.) he explains why:

O Wolkenland, zu dessen Küsten fliehen
Stets die Gedanken, suchen sie Vergessen.
O Wolken, die am Himmel einsam ziehen,
Ihr könnt allein die Einsamkeit ermessen.

His love of clouds, which is seen in poem after poem and is confirmed by the
fact that his original title for *Der ewige Tag* was *Die Wolken,* seems to go back
to about 1905. This was when he wrote his first cloud-poems. It was also at
about this time that he saw at the 12th or 13th Berliner Secession a picture
which he called 'Die Menschen unter der Wolke' (this was not its actual
title; it was probably one of Munch's pictures of anxiety); he described it in
his diary as 'eins der wenigen Bilder, die ich nie vergessen werde' (*T:*
29.9.09). Heym seems to have been fascinated by clouds because of their
beauty and ambiguity, and also to have regarded them as signs. Obvious
symbols of the passing of time, of which he was so aware, clouds represent a
higher realm of beauty, and promise escape from earth-bound misery, but
they also, and more often, mirror the scene below. Thus the first striking
cloud-description in Heym's diary — 'Im Osten war eine große Wolken-
bank, wie ein Hochgebirge mit Felswänden und Schluchten von der
untergehenden Sonne beglänzt' (*T:* 14.4.07) — is simply a reflection of the
sublimity of nature, lit by the sun which he worshipped. A number of
cloud-formations are animated. On 3 February 1908 he notes 'eine große
Wolke, gestaltet wie ein breitnackiges zu Boden schauendes Stierhaupt',
and on 30 November 1910 he writes 'Ich beobachte die Wolken, gelbliche,
weiße Fische, Fasane, eine Maus auf blauem Grund. Und rechts ein
wunderbares Phantom, wie ein riesiger Polyp mit unzähligen, langen,
feinen Armen.' Such images illustrate the tendency of Heym's imagination
to see objects in animal form, as well as recalling Nietzsche's *Also sprach
Zarathustra* (XLVIII: 'Den ziehenden Wolken bin ich gram, diesen
schleichenden Raub-Katzen: sie nehmen dir und mir, was uns gemein ist').
On another occasion the clouds are identified with the indifference of any
possible deity, good or evil:

> Der gute Gott sitzt oben hinter den Wolken und rührt sich nicht. Da ist alles Stein, taub
> hohl und leer.
>   Viel eher ist die Idee eines bösen Gottes . . . möglich . . . Warum hält sich die
> Macht immer versteckt . . .? Weil er lieblos ist, kalt und stumm wie die Wolkenbilder, die
> ewig die der Erde abgewandten Köpfe vor sich her tragen, als wüßten sie um ein
> schreckliches Geheimnis . . . (*T:* June 1910)

We shall see shortly that this 'terrible secret' probably has to do with death.
Both more typical of Heym and even more striking is another cloud-image:

> Wolken: eine ungeheure schwarze Fläche, wie ein riesiges schwarzes Land bedeckt den
> südlichen Himmel. Rechts, gen Westen, reiht sich daran ein breites, über den ganzen
> Himmel gespanntes Band, breit, tiefrot. Wie die Trauben an der Stirn eines bekränzten
> Gottes, so hängt eine Anzahl von roten langen Fetzen daraus herab.
>   Ganz oben in der Mitte ist wie ein ungeheurer Spiralnebel eine rote feine Wolke, die in
> dem tiefen Blau langsam zerfließt. Als ich diese sah, verlor ich vor Taumel fast den Boden
> unter den Füßen. (*T:* 20.9.10).

Once his imagination has seen it thus, the cloud formation becomes a
revelation, a sign to the poet from one of 'his' gods, while, in poetic terms,
this remarkable image prefigures that of 'Der Gott der Stadt' elaborated

two months later.

Heym gave clouds darker associations than did Baudelaire and Brecht, for he connected them with the dead, writing in 'Den Wolken II' (*L* 678f.):

> Der toten Geister seid ihr, die zum Flusse
> Zum überladnen Kahn der Wesenlosen
> Der Bote führt . . .

In another poem, 'Die Stadt in den Wolken' (*L* 628f.), he writes of a cloud-necropolis. This in turn suggests that when he writes of his work as 'der beste Beweis eines metaphysischen Landes, das seine schwarzen Halbinseln weit hinein in unsere flüchtigen Tage streckt' (*T:* 15.9.11), he is developing what was originally a cloud-image; the 'metaphysisches Land' with its black peninsulas is a variant of the 'riesiges schwarzes Land' of 'Die Stadt in den Wolken'. It is therefore the realm of death whose fingers or tendrils stretch down into 'unsere flüchtigen Tage'. There are poems in which the outline of those black peninsulas is clearly visible; indeed, one could say that the sharp black edge which Heym's images always possess, is part of that same outline.

The Problem of Control

'Phantasie zu haben, ist leicht. Wie schwer aber, ihre Bilder zu gestalten', Heym wrote in his diary on 20 September 1908. Leaving aside the question of whether having imagination *is* easy, Heym uses a number of techniques to give his images force and dynamism, among them personification and verbal metaphor. Personification — a kind of aesthetic primitivism — is Heym's most basic technique. It is ironical that as man is increasingly depersonalized by the hostility of his environment, the abstractions of which this hostility consists are themselves personified. As a result, man's fears become more real than anything else about him; he is overshadowed by the megapolis in which he lives, this being personified in a succession of monstrous 'deities' ('Die Dämonen der Städte,' 'Der Gott der Stadt', 'Der Krieg') and of lesser demons typical of the Gothic imagination (vampires, bats, etc.). It is the monstrousness of life, including the monstrous inhumanity of man, which such figures embody. In 'Das Fieberspital' (*L* 166-9) Fever is memorably animated into a 'gelblicher Polyp'. It was probably a cloud which he saw at this time, 'ein wunderbares Phantom, wie ein riesiger Polyp mit unzähligen, langen, feinen Armen' (*T:* 30.11.10), which gave him the fever-metaphor; we have seen how brilliantly Hunger is personified in the poem of that title.

Given the chaotic power with which Heym sees the monstrous as intervening in life, verb-metaphors are an important adjunct of his personification; it is what his demons *do* that makes them so appalling. Man is seen as unable to control his destiny, so in the later poetry the passive is used more and more as Heym sees man only as the suffering victim of a monstrous fate, which may appear in the guise of a mythical monster. The uncontrollable forces of nature are frequently given animal, monster or demon form; in his diary he wrote ' . . . steht die Qual in mir auf / Wie ein gewaltiges Tier / Das hinaus will aus mir / Denn es fraß mich schon leer' (*T:* 5.9.11). He is here re-using an image which he first used in 1905: 'immer sind da diese häßlichen Qualen wie gräuliche Spinnen, die einem alles Hohe aussaugen' (*T:* 6.11.05). In 'Die Züge' (*L* 189) there is a memorable final image — 'des Ostwinds Schnabel . . ./ Der, goldgefiedert, wie ein starker Greif, / Mit breiter Brust hinab gen Abend braust' — in which the east-wind is animated into the lion-bodied eagle (Greif) or vulture (Greifvogel). This image belongs together with a no less striking one in 'Die Schläfer' (*L* 177f.: 'Mit grünem Fittich . . . / Flattert der Schlaf, der Schnabel dunkelrot'), the effect of which is to link sleep with death. In each case the image takes us back to 'des Todes starken Vögeln' of 'Der Krieg', those imaginary but vulture-like creatures (cf. also the 'Totenvogel' of 'Die Morgue' (*L* 474-8) and the *Totenvogel* of German folklore) which are one aspect of the monster Death which is everywhere apparent in Heym's work, and which reappear in Brecht's Rimbaud-inspired early work. In another poem, 'Mors' (*L* 130ff.), Death is personified no less memorably, and in the same way:

Doch auf dem Haufen weißer Schädel thront
Der Tod im Dunkel, wie ein großer Vogel,
Der nachts bebrütet einen großen Horst.
Wie alt er ist. Wie stumm. Was mag er denken
In seines großen Schädels weißem Dach.

In 'Was kommt ihr, weiße Falter' (*L* 311f.), the conventional baroque view of life is similarly given a sharp edge of nightmare:

Ich höre oft im Schlaf der Vampire Gebell
Aus trüben Mondes Waben wie Gelächter,
Und sehe tief in leeren Höhlen
Der heimatlosen Schatten Lichter.

Was ist das Leben? Eine kurze Fackel
Umgrinst von Fratzen aus dem schwarzen Dunkel
Und manche kommen schon und strecken
Die magern Hände nach der Flamme.

At such points Heym's visions must again be compared with those of Baudelaire, in whose menagerie of the vices in the guise of reptiles the Vampires represent, as here, the agonies of the damned alive, and of Bosch. Viereck writes of Heym's 'horror that looks back to the preurban visions of

Bosch',[18] which makes good sense in terms of the horrified visions of both men; but there the resemblance stops, for Bosch was a sectarian Christian depicting the sinfulness of the world as he saw it, whereas Heym is an atheist reduced to despair by what he sees as the mousetrap of life, although it is Alfred Lichtenstein who actually uses the metaphor in his poem 'Sommerfrische' (*GG* 67): 'Friedliche Welt, du große Mausefalle, / Entkäm ich endlich dir . . . O hätt ich Flügel'. Heym not only sees the world as the domain of demons; he sees it as the creation of a demon, as a diary-entry dating from late December 1909 shows: 'Könnte man den Dämon, der sich die Welt aus den Fingern rollen ließ, einfangen, man müßte ihn in Ketten legen und auspeitschen, damit er nicht noch ein anderes Mal im Kosmos ein solches Unheil stifte.' Apart from the characteristic use of the word 'Dämon', this is a reference to the story of Brahma creating the world by mistake, mentioned by Schopenhauer in the *Nachträge zur Lehre vom Leiden der Welt*. Another memorable image of a similar kind and provenance is found in Heym's diary in March 1908: 'Der Schmerz ist wie ein Dach über der ganzen Welt. Im einzelnen Menschen baut er sich Säulen, auf denen er sich über alles Menschliche Sein hinspannt.'

The massivity of some of Heym's best poems, in which the images are crowded together in Bosch-like seeming confusion and the animal dynamism of his imagery is reinforced by the power of his rhetoric, amounts to a kind of continual overwriting, the poetic equivalent of the overstatements of the diary (when he has put his foot in it, he has to say that he has dropped the clanger of the century). His poems do indeed 'glow with primitive energy and bypassed grammar'.[19] What meant most to Heym was imaginative passion, the brainstorm of the poem's gestation. At times he was indifferent to the outcome: 'Mir erscheint ein Gedicht nur dann noch gut, wenn ich es noch nicht gemacht habe . . . Danach interessieren sie mich nicht mehr' (*T*: 22.10.10). But, like any writer worth his salt, he was also plagued by the 'Gegensatz zwischen Wollen und dem so erbärmlichen Vollbringen' (*T*: 25.5.06). The very vividness of the images in his mind must have made him feel that he had not succeeded in capturing them, particularly when one remembers that he would have liked to be able to express them in a non-verbal medium. The most important feature of his imagery is its painterly quality; images of the moon as a 'rote Sichel' or 'Geisterschiff' or 'ungeheurer Schädel, weiß und tot' are essentially visual and romantic. His images are normally less grotesque than those of Blass, Hoddis and Lichtenstein, for they are the result of sheer imagination, not of poetic *gaminerie*.

His painterly images, always vivid, sometimes lurid, 'crystallize and cluster around a central visionary focus'[20] in such a way that, like Kafka's images, they draw attention into themselves away from the world which they deny for the sake of art. And they are Kafka-like too in that Heym's suppression of the 'as if' element in his metaphors is equivalent to Kafka's use of the 'intentional symbol' in which the first part of the metaphor in question has been suppressed; in the poem 'Die Stadt' (L 452), for instance, the windows of the houses are described as animal-eyes, not as being like them. We are presented with a challengingly, chillingly 'absolute' image: it is the *reality* of those animal eyes that remains in the mind's eye. The seemingly ruthless objectivity with which Heym piles image upon image like Ossa upon Pelion is the result of moral self-control, his way of keeping at bay the demons rampaging in his head. Until his last summer he must have been afraid of his visions, forced to put a brake on them lest they run away with him. But let there be no doubt: for all its *appearance* of ruthless objectivity, Heym's work is profoundly personal, as a comparison of the imagery of the poetry and the diary quickly reveals. All his most memorable personifications (War, the God of the City, Hunger, etc). are *personae*, masks, personifications of aspects of the poet.

To Heym the accumulation of the images, or imaged lines, as they mostly are, matters more than the sequence (although the sequence may also be important, as it is to the logic of 'Der Krieg'). It is generally a spatial impression that is conveyed, not a chronological or temporal one. The poems are in effect word-paintings. It is no chance that Kirchner chose to illustrate them, although it must be said that the decadent figures, non-harmonious brushstrokes and 'unreal' colours of his Berlin paintings combine to give them the grotesque, hallucinatory quality that we associate with Hoddis and Lichtenstein rather than with Heym. This painterly emphasis on space reflects Heym's view that life is not a meaningful sequence but a miasma, Schopenhauer's whirlpool of suffering. It was the obsessive nature of his cyclopic vision that caused him to revert to the same basic forms; he was a painter of verbal images whose interest was in the canvas, not in the frame. For one form to be succeeded by another would imply a succession of different views, whereas there is in his view no such thing, for *plus ça change, plus c'est la même chose*. In his diary he made precisely this point: 'Ich glaube, daß meine Größe darin liegt, daß ich erkannt habe, es gibt wenig Nacheinander. Das meiste liegt in einer Ebene. Es ist alles ein Nebeneinander' (*T:* 21.7.10). If one takes this seriously, one can hardly say, with Stadler, that Heym lacked his own form and rhythm. In a sense his very *Unerschütterlichkeit* is his rhythm.

As man and poet Heym was faced by the same problem: the problem of control. None knew better than he did that passion, of whatever kind, is a wilful mistress and will not always be controlled ('Meine Natur sitzt wie in einer Zwangsjacke. Ich platze schon in allen Gehirnnähten' — *T:* 29.11.10). Certainly there are occasional failures of control both in his life and in his work. If he uses personification to control his perspective, he uses 'Baudelairean forms' in order to contain his visions. In 1910 he wrote a number of sonnet-sequences ('Berlin', 'Abende im Vorfrühling', 'Marathon', 'Mont St. Jean', and 'Der Spaziergang': *L passim*) in addition to many single sonnets, and could be said to have been over-attached to the sonnet-form both in the sense that many of the poems in question could equally well have been Baudelairean 16-line ones, and in the sense that he is misusing a reflective verse-form for descriptive purposes. However, such criticism is misplaced. It is more important to realize that he is all the time playing with fire in the form of that brilliant, wayward imagination. The occasional failures of control in his poetry have been well described by Philip Thomson:

> Heym takes grim, horrifying or repulsive subjects and, by imposing on them a high-powered lyrical treatment, draws them into a poetic world . . . Heym subsumes the horrifying and the ugly into a lyrical dimension . . . His best poems succeed because he is able to use violent and extreme subject-matter and style with sensitivity and control. Where the pathos and power are not sustained, however, where he lapses into clumsy and contrived diction, his poetry is grotesque [in the sense that] one's sense of the ludicrous is aroused by the clumsiness of treatment. [The] discrepancy between intention and result is comical.[21]

Such failures are, however, few and far between; much more significant is the fact that here too Heym can generally match Baudelaire, of whom Swinburne said that 'even of the loathsomest . . . putrescence and decay he can make some noble use'. The other type of 'failure' paradoxically involves too much control. Heym could, that is, be said to have failed for too long to escape from what he himself came to call the 'lie' of iambics and the 'blasphemy' of fixed rhymes, just as he could be criticized — by an insensitive critic — for writing too much too fast; he was known among his friends for his occasionally slapdash rhymes, his 'Heymerei und Reimerei' as one of them called it (*DuS*, VI, 28). His implied self-criticism, to which we shall shortly return, sounds like an expression of his exasperation with himself for producing iambics in conventionally rhymed 4-line blocks when he could have been writing more personally and in some ways more effectively in other forms, and at the same time a feeling that the form of much of his recent verse was arbitrary and superstitious rather than necessary. Two questions arise: why does so much of his work follow the same formal pattern, and should it have done so?

A brief answer to these two questions would be that the unchanging form of much of his work is a perfectly proper reflection of his view of the monotony of life, but that two facts remain: that Heym did become dissatisfied with this form, and that he writes marvellously in the last few months of his life when he lets his hair down. Since, however, this is an issue that directly affects his poetic stature, some elaboration is necessary.

There are several possible reasons for the relentless formalism or monotone of so much of his work. He may have found it difficult to escape

from the example of the coffee-house poets, who almost invariably wrote in
iambic pentameters, or of Baudelaire, or of his own work; or he may not
have wished to break the mould, either because he was afraid to do so, or
because he was satisfied with it. I am inclined to wonder whether he was not
afraid to break the mould, but there is also much to be said for the view that
it was the obsessive nature of his 'cyclopic vision' that caused him to revert
to the same basic form(s). Indeed, it has been well argued that the
practically unchanging pattern of his work from early 1910 to mid-1911 is
one of its most significant features:

> so bannt der Dichter gewaltsam alles in seine ureigenste, gebieterisch festgelegte, kaum je
> veränderte Perspektive. Unwandelbar wie diese Sehweise hält sich die künstlerische Form
> durch: die Sprache (unindividueller Wortschatz, blockhaft wuchtige Syntax) sowie das
> rhythmische und strophische Grundschema (fünfhebige Jambenverse, durch immer
> gleiche Reime fest zu Vierzeilern verbunden). Wie ein Alp legt sich unentgehbar
> die Grundstimmung solcher Verse als dumpfe Monotonie, grauenhafte Öde,
> dämonische Langeweile auf das Gemüt des Lesers.[22]

In other words, what kept coming into Heym's mind were iambic pentameter lines in 4-line blocks, and not only did his obsessive, cyclopic vision
leave him with little time or inclination to break the Baudelairean mould of
his work; it left him with no incentive for doing so since that formally
primitive monotone is the necessary expression of the monotony of life. This
is a perfectly proper argument which would, however, have been more
convincing if Heym had *not* broken the mould in September 1911.

Whatever the reason, it is a fact that until the last few months of his life he
refused to let his imagination run away with him formally and rhythmically
speaking. In his best-known work, that written between December 1909
and September 1911, there is *both* a relative lack of any 'personal rhythm'
(as Stadler noted) *and* relatively little rhythmic variation. It is, however,
important to distinguish between the rhythmic monotone of his *most typical*
work, and the rhythmic lightness of touch and variety of his early work and
his best, late work. With reference to his work as a whole it is not true to say
that his 'ear is better than his eye; his pulsations are truer than his
pictures';[23] what is true is that some of his last poems show him to have been
acquiring a marvellous ear.

Now let us come back to Heym's implied self-criticism. What he wrote in
September 1911 was: 'Der Jambus ist eine Lüge . . . In einer großen
Curve bin ich dahin zurück gekehrt, wo ich einst ausging . . . Der
gezwungene Reim ist eine Gotteslästerung, ich bin wieder bei meinen
allerersten Gedichten' (*T*: 27.9.11). These are the words of a poet who has,
for three years, written poems of one kind, only to discover, when it is too
late, that he should have been writing a different sort of poem altogether.
The evidence of the poems is clear: before December 1909 he wrote
relatively few poems in iambic pentameters, and indeed up to that point his

work is metrically very varied. From December 1909 to September 1911 he
wrote few poems that were not in iambic pentameters, and while his work
gained in power following his membership of *Der Neue Club* in Spring 1910,
one does wonder whether the influence of the Berlin literary scene was not
formally stultifying. And then, in September 1911, he had only three
months left to return to the metrical freedom and variety of his teenage
poems. Tragically, and ironically, he died just at the moment when his
imagination, including his aural imagination, had begun to revolt: 'Jetzt
habe ich den Kampf. Denn meine Phantasie ist gegen mich aufgetreten und
will nicht mehr wie ich will. Meine Phantasie, meine Seele, sie haben Angst
und rennen wie verzweifelt in ihrem Käfig. Ich kann sie nicht mehr fangen'
(*T:* 20.11.11). The upshot was both that he found himself writing more
freely and personally and beautifully than ever before, in poems like 'Deine
Wimpern, die langen' and 'Mit den fahrenden Schiffen', and that his
imagination was now prepared to assert itself to break the monotone, as it
does so dramatically in the crumbling final lines of 'Die Morgue' and the
broken cadences of 'Letzte Wache'.

'Deine Wimpern, die langen' (*L* 315f.), written in July 1911, is dedicated
to Hildegard Krohn; indeed, when it first appeared in *Die Aktion* on 12
February 1912, it bore the title 'An Hildegard K.', to which the by then
dead poet's father objected. Faced with a poem of the quality of 'Deine
Wimpern, die langen,' the critic's main aim should be to say as little as
possible. On the face of it, this is a love-poem inspired by one of several girls
with whom the poet was in love at the time; but if one reads it slowly and,
above all, if one *listens* to it, it is revealed to be something more. In a sense
most of the poem is present or prefigured in that memorable opening
stanza:

Deine Wimpern, die langen,
Deiner Augen dunkele Wasser,
Laß mich tauchen darein,
Laß mich zur Tiefe gehn.

The imagery of the poem flows with its rhymes, so that the symbolisms of
the poem intermingle. The miner goes down his shaft in an action that
parallels the lover's descent into his beloved. Both separately and together
the actions are symbolical, as rhythm and interlaced imagery show, but
ultimately the two visible symbolic planes flow into a third, invisible one,
for the falling cadence of the poem contains enough of elegiac metre to leave
one in no doubt that the poem is simultaneously a love-poem and a poem
about death. The leaf which falls on the beloved's neck at the end is a
memento mori which stands for the shadow under which man lives and the
rapidly lengthening shadow under which Heym was living. The leaf is
preceded by other shadows, the most telling of these being the shadow cast
on the near-perfect beauty of the poem by the falling cadence which makes

this lyrical celebration of love's desire into a masked elegy. Heym rarely, if ever, wrote more delicately than this. On 2 July 1910 he had what was clearly a precognitive dream about his own death eighteen months later. Many of his poems show that he was obsessed with death; his best poems on the subject are those which are simultaneously love-poems. 'Deine Wimpern, die langen' is such a poem; so, more obviously, are two other late poems in trimeters, 'Letzte Wache' and 'Mit den fahrenden Schiffen'.

In 'Deine Wimpern, die langen' there was a marvellous tension between the images of love and the cadences of death. 'Letzte Wache' (*L* 342) is wholly elegiac but breathes love. Here is what Gottfried Benn called one of the three greatest love poems ever written:

Wie dunkel sind deine Schläfen.
Und deine Hände so schwer.
Bist du schon weit von dannen,
Und hörst mich nicht mehr.

Unter dem flackenden Lichte
Bist du so traurig und alt,
Und deine Lippen sind grausam
In ewiger Starre gekrallt.

Morgen schon ist hier das Schweigen
Und vielleicht in der Luft
Noch das Rascheln von Kränzen
Und ein verwesender Duft.

Aber die Nächte werden
Leerer nun, Jahr um Jahr.
Hier wo dein Haupt lag, und leise
Immer dein Atem war.

The two central stanzas explain Peter Viereck's view that this is 'the most bluntly powerful elegy ever written in German',[24] but what stands out even more is the perfect and delicate beauty of the stanzas by which that blunt power is framed. The first and last stanzas have the kind of beautiful simplicity achieved after Heym's death first by Brecht (in his most beautiful elegy, 'Jahr für Jahr') and then by Bobrowski. It seems almost incredible that the man who produced the iambic monotone of all those black visions should suddenly have proved capable of writing some of the best trimeters in the German language. Even more incredible is the fact that there is a poem, 'Die Morgue' (*L* 474-8), written in May/June 1911, in which a seemingly endless succession of inflexible iambic pentameter quatrains finally crumbles, in the most dramatic way, into eight trimeter lines which show the poet's imagination suddenly breaking free in the extremity of his personal horror and premonition of death:

Oder — wird niemand kommen?
Und werden wir langsam zerfallen,
In dem Gelächter des Monds,
Der hoch über Wolken saust,
Zerbröckeln in Nichts,
— Daß ein Kind kann zerballen
Unsere Größe dereinst
In der dürftigen Faust?

Something similar happens, in metrical terms, between the two versions of 'Mit den fahrenden Schiffen . . . ' (*L* 456ff.), both of them written in early November 1911. The first version of the poem — it is an elegy — was written in what could be called a loosely 'elegiac' pattern; the predominantly dactylic lines started by being mostly pentameters, and ended by being mostly hexameters. In rewriting the poem Heym has given his metrical imagination its head, and has cut the six-beat lines in half (cf. Rilke's procedure with the sonnet-form), so that again we have a poem in the by now familiar, basically dactylic trimeter pattern. The result is a revelation, a poem which is lighter, more lucid, and more deeply elegiac:

Mit den fahrenden Schiffen
Sind wir vorübergeschweift,
Die wir ewig herunter
Durch glänzende Winter gestreift.
Ferner kamen wir immer
Und tanzten im insligen Meer,
Weit ging die Flut uns vorbei,
Und Himmel war schallend und leer.

Sage die Stadt,
Wo ich nicht saß im Tor,
Ging dein Fuß da hindurch,
Der die Locke ich schor?
Unter dem sterbenden Abend
Das suchende Licht
Hielt ich, wer kam da hinab,
Ach, ewig in fremdes Gesicht.

Bei den Toten ich rief,
Im abgeschiedenen Ort,
Wo die Begrabenen wohnen;
Du, ach, warest nicht dort.
Und ich ging über Feld,
Und die wehenden Bäume zu Haupt
Standen im frierenden Himmel
Und waren im Winter entlaubt.

Raben und Krähen
Habe ich ausgesandt,
Und sie stoben im Grauen
Über das ziehende Land.
Aber sie fielen wie Steine
Zur Nacht mit traurigem Laut
Und hielten im eisernen Schnabel
Die Kränze von Stroh und Kraut.
Manchmal ist deine Stimme,
Die im Winde verstreicht,
Deine Hand, die im Traume
Rühret die Schläfe mir leicht;
Alles war schon vorzeiten.
Und kehret wieder sich um.
Gehet in Trauer gehüllet,
Streuet Asche herum.

It is tragic that Heym died just at the moment when he found himself writing poems like 'Deine Wimpern, die langen' and 'Mit den fahrenden Schiffen'. Such poems show him reverting to the type of poem he had written at the beginning of his poetic career under the influence of Hölderlin. Had he lived longer, his formal range would unquestionably have become wider as his despair deepened.

Emmy Ball-Hennings commented (*DuS*, VI, 90) that Heym was half rowdy, half angel. The poems for which he has become known are the work of the brilliantly gifted rowdy; the marvellous series of trimeter elegies and near-elegies dating from his last months are the work of the angel. When his reputation has settled down and he has been detached from the 'Expressionism' to which he does not belong in any very useful sense, it is likely that these last poems will be regarded as his major contribution to German poetry. There is no doubt in my mind that he is one of the greatest German elegiac poets.

II   The Poet as Clown: Alfred Lichtenstein

A Man Apart

Although his collected poems were republished in 1966, the work of Alfred Lichtenstein is today — with the exception of one single poem — less known than ever. The rediscovery of poetic Expressionism is no doubt partly responsible for this neglect in that Lichtenstein has suffered from being considered solely in the context of a style which he outgrew. It is wrong that a writer of his quality, originality and importance (which has relatively little to do with Expressionism as such) should be forgotten.

Lichtenstein began his *curriculum vitae* with the words 'Ich, Alfred Lichtenstein, bin am 23.VIII.1889 als Sohn des Fabrikanten David Lichtenstein zu Berlin geboren. Meine Religionsangehörigkeit ist die jüdische. Ich bin Preuße.' The irony which is so characteristic of his work is already in evidence here: anything less like a 'Prussian' is hard to imagine. The other salient facts of his short life can be given briefly. On leaving the Luisenstädtisches Gymnasium, he proceeded to read Law at the universities of Berlin and Erlangen, graduating with a doctoral thesis on *Die rechtswidrige öffentliche Aufführung von Bühnenwerken* (publ. Berlin, 1913). Following his graduation he joined the 2nd Royal Bavarian Infantry Regiment for one year of military service. Within the year the First World War had broken out and he had died in agony. He began writing poetry at school and began to attract attention during his student years, but quite properly and with characteristic honesty regarded most of his first two or three years' production as unimportant. His first published poem appeared in *Der Sturm* on 24 November 1910, after which his work also appeared in *Simplicissimus, Die Aktion, Pan*, etc. Although much of his work appeared in *Die Aktion* (the leading outlet for radically experimental poetry, which published a Lichtenstein-number on 4 October 1913), the satirical journal *Simplicissimus* was arguably a more appropriate forum for it. His first book publication was *Die Geschichten des Onkel Krause* (1910). A pamphlet collection of twenty of his poems was published by A.R. Meyer in 1913 under the title *Die Dämmerung*. In October of the same year a group of fourteen poems appeared in *Die Aktion*. He died of a stomach wound near Rheims on 25 September 1914; like Heym, he seems to have foreseen his death. His collected poems and prose sketches (*Gedichte und Geschichten*, ed. Kurt Lubasch) appeared in two volumes in 1919. His *Gesammelte Gedichte* appeared in 1962 and his *Gesammelte Prosa* in 1966. Part of his *Nachlaß* is deposited in the library of the Free University of Berlin; the rest was destroyed during the Second World War.

In a prose sketch, 'Mieze Meier', published in *Der Sturm* on 8 September 1910, Lichtenstein wrote: 'Ich besuche noch das Gymnasium, doch interessiere ich mich mehr für Theater und Literatur. Ich lese Wedekind, Rilke und andere. Auch Goethe. Schiller und George mag ich nicht.' (*GP* 9). It was perhaps inevitable that the young Lichtenstein would be impressed by the work of Rilke and Hofmannsthal, although he quickly grew out of Rilke and was never really influenced by Hofmannsthal, whom he echoes in a few poems, most interestingly in 'Die Plagiatoren' (5.1. 1912: *GG* 36). It was certainly inevitable that he would share Heym's distaste for anything smacking of pomposity. Like his favourite poets, Wedekind and Heine, Lichtenstein had *esprit*. He is a master of the slyly comic phrase. Even at school he was noted for his penchant for witty, off-beat formulations, and Alfred Kerr, who published some of Lichtenstein's work in his periodical *Pan,* called him the 'tollste komische Kraft seit Wedekind', adding: 'Ich schrie vor seinen Manuskripten und sank vom Stuhl.'[25] It was no chance that some of his earlier poems first appeared in Wedekind's forum (*Simplicissimus*). From Wedekind he got his cabaret-tone. Other poets who left their mark on his work were Baudelaire (urban imagery), Verlaine (mixed registers) and, most importantly, Laforgue (irony). In the case of Laforgue it is a question not merely of irony, including self-mockery, but of something wider and more elusive, something described by Arthur Symons in such a way as to be immediately applicable to Lichtenstein:

> Verse and prose are alike a kind of travesty, making subtle use of colloquialism, slang, neologism . . . for their allusive, their factitious, their reflected meanings . . . The verse is alert, troubled, swaying, deliberately uncertain, hating rhetoric so piously that it prefers, and finds its piquancy in, the ridiculously obvious.[26]

The major influence was, however, Heinrich Heine, although this has yet to be recognized; Lichtenstein does not mention Heine in 'Mieze Meier'. What he has in common with Heine is his 'stimmungszerstörende Ironie',[27] the 'Lust auf Destruktion des verlogen Harmonischen',[28] the mixture of romanticism and knowing anti-romanticism, the occasional use of the *Heine-Strophe,* and, above all, the rapid changes of register and the shock-effects thus produced. More generally he shares with Heine an ironical Jewish consciousness, a sense of alienation, and a mordant, off-beat, irreverent wit. He is a Heine-like romantic (as opposed to the Hölderlin-like romantic Georg Heym) whose attitude to himself and to his own romanticism is ironical or knowing; he is a complex, Chaplinesque figure, whose sphere is tragicomedy. Like Heine, and like Heym, he is something of a split personality; but if Heym's prime characteristic is passion, Lichtenstein's is irony. Like Heym he can be as melancholy as a dog. His attitude is self-belittling, hence his *persona,* the crazy dwarf Kuno Kohn, to whom we shall return. The influence on his poetic development of Jakob van Hoddis (the 'Max Mechenmal' of the 'Café Klößchen' sketches) will be discussed presently, and his prose work would have been very different if it had not been for the influence of Paul Scheerbart's *Ich liebe Dich! Ein Eisenbahnroman mit 66 Intermezzos* (1897) and Carl Einstein's *Bebuquin* (1912; part publication in *Opale*, 1907).

Known to his friends as a clown, a wit, a man apart, a marked man, a man with a love of nonsense, a profound sense of the absurdity of the world and the 'black' humour that so often goes with this, Lichtenstein was a man of many parts in more senses than one; his literary *personae* included 'Onkel Krause', 'Aliwi' and 'Kuno Kohn'. That he wrote poetry of several kinds, is therefore hardly surprising. In *Die Aktion*, on 4 October 1913, Lichtenstein himself distinguished between three types of poem he had written up to then:

> Die folgenden Gedichte können in drei Gruppen geteilt werden. Eine vereinigt phantastis-che, halb spielerische Gebilde: Der Traurige. Die Gummischuhe. Capriccio. Der Lack-schuh. Wüstes Schimpfen eines Wirtes . . . Das früheste Gedicht einer zweiten Gruppe ist Die Dämmerung. Daß Die Dämmerung und andere Gedichte die Dinge komisch nehmen (das Komische wird tragisch empfunden. Die Darstellung ist . . . 'grotesk'), das Unausgeglichene, nicht Zusammengehörige der Dinge, das Zufällige, das Durcheinander bemerken . . . ist jedenfalls nicht das Charakteristische des 'Stils' . . . Auch andere Verschiedenheiten zwischen älteren Gedichten (z.B. Die Dämmerung) und später ent-standenen (z.B. Die Angst) Gedichten desselben Stils sind nachweisbar. Man möge beachten, daß immer häufiger besondersartige Reflexionen das Landschaftsbild scheinbar durchbrechen. Wohl nicht ohne bestimmte künstlerische Absichten. Die dritte Gruppe sind die Gedichte des Kuno Kohn.

Though interesting, this is also — or so it seems to me — deliberately misleading. Certainly critics have been misled by it into making distinc-tions which serve only to obscure Lichtenstein's *development* as a poet and therefore his importance. All his work is personal, idiosyncratic, 'fantastic' and to some extent 'playful', but it also develops, particularly from 1912 onwards. 'Die Dämmerung', written on 5 March 1911, was initially something of a flash in the pan, for it was not until about a year later that Lichtenstein began to produce other *good* poems of this type. With the exception of 'Die Dämmerung', nearly all his stronger poems were written in 1912-14; the best were unquestionably written in the last weeks of his life (these were war-poems, certainly, but they were also poems in a new style). It is therefore more appropriate to treat his poems on a mainly chronologic-al basis, for in this way both his development and his very considerable contribution to German poetry will become clear.

Lichtenstein himself rejected most of his 'ersten achtzig Gedichte' (i.e. most of the poems written before 'Die Dämmerung', which was No. 85 in his *oeuvre*) as 'unbedeutend' because conventional in theme and somewhat aggressive in expression:

Der Inhalt ist die Not der Liebe, des Todes, der allgemeinen Sehnsucht. So weit sie 'zynisch' (im Kabaretton) sind, mag beispielsweise der Wunsch, sich überlegen zu fühlen, den Anstoß zu ihrer Formulierung gegeben haben. (*Gedichte*, 1919, 3)

Certainly the poet was an outsider, and no doubt he felt insecure; but there is much more to his early poetry than that or the fact that some of his characteristic forms and themes can be found there. What is much more to the point is the fact that his early work includes some remarkable poems, notably the cabaret-ballad-type *Ich-Gedichte* 'Man hat mich glücklich eingesperrt . . . ' and 'Komisches Lied'.

In the first of these Lichtenstein's typical ironical tone is immediately heard in lines, reminiscent of Wedekind, which show his self-deprecating yet serious attitude to his work:

> Man hat mich glücklich eingesperrt,
> Dran ist mir nichts gelegen,
> Und für total verrückt erklärt
> Des Dichtens nämlich wegen.

> (*GG* 13f.)

We shall return presently to the question of the poet's 'craziness'; for the present it is sufficient to enjoy his crazy doggerel.

'Komisches Lied' was written as a riposte to 'Was ich liebe' by the Jewish 'decadent' poet Felix Dörmann (pseudonym for Felix Biedermann, 1870-1928), author of the scandalous collections *Neurotica* (1891), *Sensationen* (1892) and *Gelächter* (1895), as the following juxtaposition makes clear. Dörmann's poem begins:

> Ich liebe die hektischen, schlanken
> Narzissen mit blutrotem Mund;
> ich liebe die Qualengedanken,
> die Herzen, zerstochen und wund.

Lichtenstein's riposte, which is dedicated to Dörmann, begins as follows:

> Ich hasse die farblose Feinheit
> Erklügelter Nervenkultur.
> Ich liebe die bunte Gemeinheit
> Der schamlosen, nackten Natur.

> (*GG* 151)

'Komisches Lied' makes clear not only Lichtenstein's dislike of 'erklügelte Nervenkultur', which explains his attitude to Stefan George, but also his opposition to the decadence which pervades his urban poems; it shows his humanity and, above all, his comic gift. The poetic career of his *persona*, Kuno Kohn, which in some ways closely parallels his own, begins with the reading of a comparable poem, 'Der Komiker'.

Die Dämmerung

Lichtenstein is today known for one poem, 'Die Dämmerung', which has attracted attention because it was the second expressionist collage-type *Zeilengedicht* to appear in print, and because it is based on the first such poem, Jakob van Hoddis's 'Weltende'. Lichtenstein wrote 'Die Dämmerung' on 5 March 1911; when the poem was printed in *Die Aktion* in October 1913, Franz Pfemfert appended to it a note reading:

Man erinnere sich des schönen: Weltende . . . des Jacob van Hoddis . . . Tatsache ist, daß A.Li. (Wi:) dies Gedicht gelesen hatte, bevor er selbst 'Derartiges' schrieb. Ich glaube also, daß van Hoddis das Verdienst hat, diesen 'Stil' gefunden zu haben, Li. das geringere, ihn ausgebildet, bereichert, zur Geltung gebracht zu haben.

That Lichtenstein was impressed by 'Weltende' is confirmed by his imitation of it, entitled 'Der Sturm', written in January 1914. Before we can assess 'Die Dämmerung', we therefore need to examine Hoddis's now famous poem:

Dem Bürger fliegt vom spitzen Kopf der Hut,
in allen Lüften hallt es wie Geschrei.
Dachdecker stürzen ab und gehn entzwei
und an den Küsten — liest man — steigt die Flut.

Der Sturm ist da, die wilden Meere hupfen
an Land, um dicke Dämme zu zerdrücken.
Die meisten Menschen haben einen Schnupfen.
Die Eisenbahnen fallen von den Brücken.

What immediately strikes one is the grotesque contrast between the staid, stuffy, conventional structure of the poem and its startling, shocking imagery. Structurally 'Weltende' looks like nothing so much as a caricature of the conventional poem: those stilted iambic pentameters, the 4-line stanza form, the stale embrace of the abba rhymes in the first stanza, the trite discordance of the cdcd rhymes in the second stanza, the faded alternation of masculine endings in the first stanza and feminine endings in the second, and so on. Formally the poem is rooted in a tradition which is challenged and indeed shattered by the collage of apparently incongruous images.

The images need to be examined closely. The first line of the first stanza reduces the normally staid 'Bürger' to a figure of fun by showing him robbed of his dignity (his hat) by a playful, irresponsible, indeed revolutionary ('spitzbübisch') wind. One thinks, inevitably, of Wedekind's 'Ein politisch Lied', which appeared in *Simplicissimus* and which contained these lines:

Nein, Ruhe ist des Bürgers erste Pflicht;
Deswegen weich ich nicht und wank ich nicht,
Und bleibe treu dem Grundsatz meiner Väter:
Wer mich beunruhigt, ist ein Hochverräter!

For a 'Spitzkopf' — which the 'Bürger' is implied to be — such a loss of dignity, of face, is the 'end of the world'. This gives us one connotation of Hoddis's title, which is by no means as obvious as it has been taken to be. The colloquial language of the first line gives way, in the second, to a more elevated tone that has a clear Biblical ring and therefore suggests that what is happening is not just 'the end', but the apocalypse. It may simply be the wind that is howling, but the wording makes one uneasy. The poem is already both funny and uncomfortable; the reader begins to be in the same position as the 'Bürger'. And now the pattern repeats itself: line 3 is ludicrously colloquial, while line 4 has distant Biblical connotations. The slaters suffer a similar fate to the 'Bürger', but in an intensified form. No doubt slaters have occasionally been blown off roofs by abnormally high winds, and when this has happened, they have no doubt sometimes met their death, an idea for which here are many comic conventional euphemisms. Hoddis's use of the verb 'entzweigehen' is ridiculous: it turns the slaters into broken dolls or puppets, while at the same time slyly suggesting that it somehow serves them right for being so absurdly careless. In fact it is a matter of human fragility, human frailty; comedy and tragedy are fused in the verb. In line 4 there is an ironical contrast between cataclysmic disaster and the civilization which is powerless to prevent it and is indeed ultimately the cause of it. The tide that is rising so sinisterly taunts the reader with its ambiguous pointer to the Flood. Whatever else it was, the Flood was not funny (neither is a tide rising out of control); presented as one macabre fact among others in the daily press, it is not tragic either, just something happening to other people, with the implication of 'Merde à ces chiens-là' (Rimbaud).

    In the second stanza the pattern changes: the rhymes are now feminine and at cross purposes. The world over which man has lost control is now predominant. The first line names the increasingly apocalyptic storm which we saw raging in the first stanza. The verb 'hupfen' again implies a playful, irresponsible action; but the action is made profoundly worrying by the reference to the Flood and the way in which the raging seas crush man's proud creations (those 'dicke Dämme') to total insignificance. In the first stanza it was the bourgeois and the workman who were reduced to figures of fun; now it is man as such who is cut down to size by an invisible, microscopic virus. Line 3 also sustains the comic note; comic is not only the idea of 'mostpeople' (to use E.E. Cumming's appropriate term) running around with luminous, dripping noses, but also the incongruity of this with the rest of the stanza. The last line contains a final notable image. The trains which unaccountably fall off bridges not only repeat, in an intensified form, the image of the slaters falling off roofs; they also recall a drawing by Bruno Paul, entitled 'Das Schreckgespenst des Herrn von Thielen', which appeared in *Simplicissimus;* the drawing showed a gigantic hound devouring a train.

Hoddis's poem consists, then, of a series of images, mostly derived from contemporary reality, which add up to anything but a realistic picture. As has been said before, the picture in question is a new and original one in that the images, however 'realistic' they may individually be, are ones that are not normally found together at the same time and place. The ironization or alienation involved in the phrasing adds a significant element to the picture, which is that of a world fast slipping out of control, a world in which abnormality is threatening to become the rule. The title of the poem has apocalyptic connotations, certainly, but the somewhat unusual German word refers, I suggest, to the end of a specific world, of a way of life, of old certainties, old safeties — it refers, in other words, to precisely what the events of the next few years were to betoken. It is a poem about how exposed man is once the accepted certainties and verities begin to crumble away. It is a poem about the finiteness, contingency and fragility of the supposed master of the natural world. It is, accordingly, a poem which has become truer and more relevant in the half-century since it was written. But to summarize it thus is to emphasize the tragic perceptions of the poem at the expense of the comic. What makes the poem so typical of its time, and indeed of Berlin at this time, is its tragi-comic nature, and, above all, the cynical insouciance which informs it. It is not only man that is cut down to size; so too are the disasters, which are trivialized and distanced, partly by being juxtaposed with trivial events, partly by being presented as *faits divers* in the newspaper (the essence of this early collage-style), and partly by the poet's unfeeling tone. It is a deliberately flat poem (*all* the feet in the last two lines end in -en!) that does not give a damn. It is an anti-poem.

The effect of this poem on Hoddis' contemporaries was later brilliantly described by Johannes R. Becher:

Meine poetische Kraft reicht nicht aus, um die Wirkung jenes Gedichtes wiederherzustellen, von dem ich jetzt sprechen will. Auch die kühnste Phantasie meiner Leser würde ich überanstrengen bei dem Versuch, ihnen die Zauberhaftigkeit zu schildern, wie sie dieses Gedicht 'Weltende' von Jakob van Hoddis für uns in sich barg. Diese zwei Strophen, o diese acht Zeilen schienen uns in andere Menschen verwandelt zu haben, uns emporgehoben zu haben aus einer Welt stumpfer Bürgerlichkeit, die wir verachteten, und von der wir nicht wußten, wie wir sie verlassen sollten. Diese acht Zeilen entführten uns. Immer neue Schönheiten entdeckten wir in diesen acht Zeilen, wir sangen sie, wir summten sie, wir murmelten sie, wir pfiffen sie vor uns hin, wir gingen mit diesen acht Zeilen auf den Lippen in die Kirchen, und wir saßen, sie vor uns hinflüsternd, mit ihnen beim Radrennen. Wir riefen sie uns gegenseitig über die Straße hinweg zu wie Losungen, wir saßen mit diesen acht Zeilen beieinander, frierend, und hungernd, und sprachen sie gegenseitig vor uns hin, und Hunger und Kälte waren nicht mehr . . . Wir fühlten uns wie neue Menschen, wie Menschen am ersten geschichtlichen Schöpfungstag, eine neue Welt sollte mit uns beginnen, und eine Unruhe, schworen wir uns, zu stiften, daß den Bürgern Hören und Sehen vergehen sollte und sie es geradezu als eine Gnade betrachten würden, von uns in den Orkus geschickt zu werden.[29]

Now it has long been known that Hoddis's 'Weltende' provided Lichtenstein with a model for 'Die Dämmerung'; what has not been realized is that
Hoddis's poem may also have had a model. This is Ernst Blass's 'Berliner
Abendstimmung', which appeared in *Der Sturm* on 24 November 1910. It
reads as follows:

Stumm wurden längst die Polizeifanfaren,
Die hier am Tage den Verkehr geregelt.
In süßen Nebel liegen hingeflegelt
Die Lichter, die am Tag geschäftlich waren.

An Häusern sind sehr kitschige Figuren.
Wir treffen manche Herren von der Presse
Und viele von den aufgebauschten Huren,
Sadistenzüge um die feine Fresse.

O komm! o komm, Geliebte! In der Bar
Verrät der Mixer den geheimsten Tip,
Und überirdisch, himmlisch steht dein Haar
Zur Rötlicheit des Cherry-Brandy Flip.

Many, though not all, of the techniques which Hoddis was to employ, are
already used by Blass. Here already are the po-faced use of the traditional
iambic pentameter and the traditional quatrain, combined with the jingling
rhythm and grotesque rhymes characteristic of the cabaret-song. This is,
then, a poem which points the finger of fun at the traditional lyric. Blass's
poem is already a collage, although he does not go so far as Hoddis and
Lichtenstein, who tend to have a new image or scene-fragment in every line.
His images constitute a grotesque world, although he does not use them
purposefully to express the idea of absurdity as such, and his poem therefore
lacks the metaphysical edge and the multidimensionality of Hoddis'
'Weltende' and Lichtenstein's 'Die Dämmerung'. But just as Hoddis must
be given credit for inspiring Lichtenstein's poem, so too must Blass be given
credit for inspiring Hodis' poem.

Lichtenstein's 'Die Dämmerung' is clearly a poem of a similar kind to
Hoddis's 'Weltende':

Ein dicker Junge spielt mit einem Teich.
Der Wind hat sich in einem Baum gefangen.
Der Himmel sieht verbummelt aus und bleich,
Als wäre ihm die Schminke ausgegangen.

Auf lange Krücken schief herabgebückt
Und schwatzend kriechen auf dem Feld zwei Lahme.
Ein blonder Dichter wird vielleicht verrückt.
Ein Pferdchen stolpert über eine Dame.

An einem Fenster klebt ein fetter Mann.
Ein Jüngling will ein weiches Weib besuchen.

Ein grauer Clown zieht sich die Stiefel an.
Ein Kinderwagen schreit und Hunde fluchen.

(*GG* 44)

It is normally argued that Lichtenstein's poem is more subtle, his ambiguous title allowing his images to 'speak for themselves'; but while his title sounds more ambiguous than Hoddis's, it is in fact only ambiguous in a more obvious way, for we assume 'Dämmerung' to mean dusk, and probably assume that this dusk has a cosmic dimension. We can come back to the title. Let us first look at his poem. As in 'Weltende', the safe, time-hallowed form is blown open by a string of amazing images. Why the various things and actions in the poem are so, we are not told; how the images are linked, we are naturally not told in the poem, although when it appeared in *Die Aktion* on 4 October 1913, Lichtenstein did 'explain' it to his readers. This is what he wrote:

Absicht ist, die Unterschiede der Zeit und des Raumes zugunsten der Idee zu beseitigen. Das Gedicht will die Einwirkung der Dämmerung auf die Landschaft darstellen. In diesem Fall ist die Einheit der Zeit bis zu einem gewissen Grade notwendig. Die Einheit des Raumes ist nicht erforderlich, deshalb nicht beachtet. In den zwölf Zeilen ist die Dämmerung am Teich, am Baum, am Feld, am Fenster, irgendwo — in ihrer Einwirkung auf die Erscheinung eines Jungen, eines Windes, eines Himmels, zweier Lahmer, eines Dichters, eines Pferdes, einer Dame, eines Mannes, eines Jünglings, eines Weibes, eines Clowns, eines Kinderwagens, einiger Hunde — bildhaft dargestellt. (Der Ausdruck ist schlecht, aber ich finde keinen besseren.)

Der Urheber des Gedichtes will nicht eine als real denkbare Landschaft geben. Vorzug der Dichtkunst vor der Malkunst ist, daß sie 'ideeliche' Bilder hat. Das bedeutet — angewandt auf die Dämmerung: Der dicke Knabe, der den großen Teich als Spielzeug benutzt und die beiden Lahmen auf Krücken über dem Feld und die Dame in einer Straße der Stadt, die von einem Wagenpferd im Halbdunkel umgestoßen wird, und der Dichter, der voll verzweifelter Sehnsucht in den Abend sinnt (wahrscheinlich aus einer Dachluke), und der Zirkusclown, der sich in dem grauen Hinterhaus seufzend die Stiefel anzieht, um pünktlich zu der Vorstellung zu kommen, in der er lustig sein muß — können ein dichterisches 'Bild' hergeben, obwohl sie malerisch nicht komponierbar sind. Die meisten leugnen das noch, erkennen daher beispielsweise in der Dämmerung und ähnlichen Gebilden nichts als ein sinnloses Durcheinander komischer Vorstellungen. Andere glauben sogar — zu unrecht —, daß auch in der Malerei derartige 'ideeliche' Bilder möglich sind. (Man denke an die Futuristenmanschepansche.)

Absicht ist weiterhin, die Reflexe der Dinge unmittelbar — ohne *überflüssige* Reflexionen aufzunehmen. Lichtenstein weiß, daß der Mann nicht an dem Fenster klebt, sondern hinter ihm steht. Daß nicht der Kinderwagen schreit, sondern das Kind in dem Kinderwagen. Da er nur den Kinderwagen sieht, schreibt er: Der Kinderwagen schreit. Lyrisch unwahr wäre, wenn er schriebe: Ein Mann steht hinter einem Fenster.

Zufällig auch begrifflich nicht unwahr ist: Ein Junge spielt *mit* einem Teich. Ein Pferd *stolpert* über eine Dame. Hunde *fluchen*. Zwar muß man sonderbar lachen, wenn man *sehen* lernt: Daß ein Junge einen Teich tatsächlich als Spielzeug benutzt. Wie Pferde die hilflose Bewegung des Stolperns haben — Wie menschlich Hunde der Wut Ausdruck geben —

Zuweilen ist die Darstellung der Reflexion wichtig. Ein Dichter wird vielleicht verrückt — macht einen tieferen Eindruck als: Ein Dichter sieht starr vor sich hin . . .

The poet's reading of his work is for the most part teasingly literal. It is all, he says, a matter of 'die Einwirkung der Dämmerung auf die Landschaft', all a matter of how things appear in the dusk (as it is confirmed to be). If this were all there is to it, he would have written a weaker poem than Hoddis. It is only because his remarks do not exhaust the meanings of his poem, that it can be argued to be even better than Hoddis's. To justify this statement, let us look closely at his images.

The fat boy — Billy Bunter — is traditionally a figure of fun; but in the opening line it is the pond which is ridiculed by means of that masterly preposition 'mit'. Other prepositions would have been factual; 'mit' amounts to an implied comment on the absurdity of life. The pond is made to look silly by being 'played with' by a fat boy. It is not the sort of thing that self-respecting ponds should put up with, not the sort of thing that Mother Nature should allow or, indeed, used to allow. But then this is the point: Mother Nature is seen as losing her grip. The wind has been careless enough to get caught in a tree, for all the world like a cat, and the sky — the very heavens, nay Heaven itself — looks pale and dissolute, 'as though it had run out of make-up.' Nature, in other words, is being treated in the same disrespectful, shocking, modernistic way as in 'The Love Song of J. Alfred Prufrock' ('When the evening is spread out against the sky / Like a patient etherized upon a table') of 1917. We shall see that this is highly characteristic of the poet at this stage of his development, but there is also a more general point involved here: the ironization of poetic forms and conventions which was a feature of the work of the *Kaffeehausliteraten*. This ironical treatment is seen not only in the parodies and pastiches which were common at the time, but also in the use of imagery which travesties conventional imagery. Thus Lichtenstein writes of 'die fette Nebelspinne', while Hoddis transmogrifies rosy-fingered Dawn into a fat old washerwoman with red, chilblained fingers, and describes the moon as 'meine Tante' and the sun as a 'fette Feuerglatze'. While readers will again think of Jules Laforgue here, let us not forget that in an earlier age of wit John Donne, in his 'The Sun Rising', wrote of the sun as a 'Busie old foole'.

In the second stanza the two lame men on their crutches are, similarly, made to appear ridiculous by the use of the verb 'kriechen'; to say that they appear foreshortened in the dusk is less than half the point. The fair-haired poet is, of course, Lichtenstein himself, whose 'crazy' imagination is at work and whose sense of the absurd is the real point of the poem. The lady knocked down by a clumsy clot of a horse loses her dignity as well as her footing. The fat man of the last stanza is described as sticking to a window not merely because of the half-light, but, above all, because of the poet's perspective. The alienation is achieved by suppression of the expected 'wie'. The youth who 'will ein weiches Weib besuchen' (splendid epithet!) is Lichtenstein himself (cf. the poem 'Nächtliches Abenteuer' of 18 November

1908). He may write of a circus clown, but one has the impression that the 'grauer Clown' is also the poet himself, the buffoon who was soon to go to his death in field-grey. The pram whose occupant cannot be seen and which therefore appears to be screaming itself, and the dogs who sound as though they are cursing (who is to say they are not?), embody the poet's droll point of view. Lichtenstein rightly went on to write, apropos this and similar poems, that 'Die Darstellung ist "grotesk"', meaning that what is 'grotesque' or 'absurd' is the way in which the thing is expressed, which in turn means the way in which the thing is travestied or mocked. And, as 'Berthold Bryller' (=Kurt Hiller) was made to say of 'Kuno Kohn's' work, the grotesque may start people thinking ('Groteske sei immerhin eine Brücke zu einem Weg' : GP, 63).

In the case of 'Die Dämmerung' the end, the whole point of the poem is its ambiguity: the ambiguous time of day pointing to the greater ambiguity surrounding life and history; the way in which things can be seen in different ways; the way in which comedy and tragedy open out from one another; and so on. Above all the poem aims to convey the poet's sense of the absurd. It is a good poem because the new, off-beat attitude is expressed in te·ms which seem appropriate to the point of inevitability. There is, one feels, no better way in which the absurdity of life could be expressed.

'Die Dämmerung' is an important historical document, although its very historical importance has, ironically, distracted attention from Lichtenstein's real poetic achievement. Even in his lifetime, 'Die Dämmerung' was overrated, though not by those who knew his work and the contemporary poetic scene best. 'Man hält Ihre Dichtungen von der Art der "Dämmerung" für Ihre wesentliche Kundgebung, obwohl es doch nur Ihre genialste war', Alfred Lemm wrote to the by then dead poet in a letter published in Die Weißen Blätter in June 1915 which shows greater understanding of Lichtenstein's work than any other contemporary document. 'Die Dämmerung' is also an original poem; confirmation of this comes, indirectly, from a pastiche of 'Weltende' entitled 'Der Sturm' (1.1.1914: GG 70), which Lichtenstein wrote at the end of his first three months in the army. During his basic training he was, not surprisingly, unable to write at all. 'Der Sturm' therefore amounts to a five-finger-exercise; but the fact that he chose to get his hand in again by writing a pastiche of 'Weltende', shows how much he had made Hoddis's style his own, even if he had by then outgrown it.

His discovery of Hoddis's poem was a turning-point in his poetic development. The point has been well made by Joachim Schreck:

Dieses Gedicht ['Weltende'] hatte für Lichtenstein eine Art katalytische Bedeutung. Lichtensteins sentimentale Ich-Lyrik der Frühzeit und seine sichtlich von Wedekind geprägte Kabarettlyrik werden durch van Hoddis' stilbildende Tat gleichsam verwandelt. Es beginnt eine neue, die wesentliche dichterische Phase Lichtensteins, in der er mit Hilfe des 'Zeilenstils' einen eigenen Ton findet.[30]

It was, paradoxically, Lichtenstein's discovery of Hoddis that caused him to find his own voice. 'Weltende' was so important to him because it gave him a form of poem and a style which for a time suited him down to the ground as a way of combining the cabaret-ballad with his characteristic fantasy, which appears in the imagery. It was no doubt because the style in question lent itself to facile superficialities, that 'Die Dämmerung' initially remained a flash in the pan.

Town and Clown

Lichtenstein himself drew attention to 'das Unausgeglichene, nicht Zusammengehörige der Dinge, das Zufällige, das Durcheinander' in poems of the 'Dämmerung'-type, although he also stressed that such things are 'nicht das Charakteristische des "Stils"'. While not all such poems reveal the grotesque face of life as seen by Lichtenstein, most of them do; the grotesque is generally present in one form or another, most often in the form of metaphor. It is the polarity of the man and his work that stands out: the way in which the poems mix real and surreal, commonplace and grotesque, objective and subjective elements; the way in which landscape or cityscape is ironized by what Lichtenstein calls the 'immer häufiger besondersartige Reflexionen' which 'das Landschaftsbild scheinbar durchbrechen'; the mixed key, the mixed register. This polarity in the work reflects the dichotomy within the poet, who can as easily be tender, romantic and composed, as he can be bitingly satirical, although it must be added that his rather shy tenderness is normally distanced by being attributed to 'Kuno Kohn', and that in *Die Dämmerung* as a whole it is satire that predominates. Irony, including self-parody, is the chief characteristic of his work. It has been admirably described by Michael Hamburger:

> Lichtenstein's irony was a considerable advance on that of earlier poets; though not free from the self-mockery made familiar by Heine and . . . Laforgue, he used the very same ironic effects to mock a whole civilization, without recourse to direct or didactic statement . . . The poems of Lichtenstein and Hoddis are distinguished by an irony which has the dual purpose of satirizing contemporary civilization and of expressing a *malaise*, a premonition of doom, which was one of the common premises of all the early Expressionists.[31]

Of course, Heine too mocked a society and a nation through irony, and Lichtenstein's self-ironization ('Ein blonder Dichter wird vielleicht verrückt'), far from being a weakness, is one of his great strengths. All his work, even his war-poetry, gains very considerably from his refusal to be seen to be taking himself too seriously. *Wichtigtuerei* is totally alien to his nature. Of how many poets can this be said?

Lichtenstein wrote more poems of the 'Dämmerung'-type than of any

other. The quality varies considerably; sometimes the images seem whimsical, not infrequently they are not sustained. The stronger poems include
'Der Winter', first published, like so many poems of this group, in *Die Aktion*
(on 26 June 1912):

> Von einer Brücke schreit vergrämt ein Hund
> Zum Himmel . . . der wie alter grauer Stein
> Auf fernen Häusern steht. Und wie ein Tau
> Aus Teer liegt auf dem Schnee ein toter Fluß.
>
> Drei Bäume, schwarzgefrorne Flammen, drohn
> Am Ende aller Erde. Stechen scharf
> Mit spitzen Messern in die harte Luft,
> In der ein Vogelfetzen einsam hängt.
>
> Ein paar Laternen waten zu der Stadt,
> Erloschne Leichenkerzen. Und ein Fleck
> Aus Menschen schrumpft zusammen und ist bald
> Ertrunken in dem schmählich weißen Sumpf.
>
> (*GG* 50)

This seems, initially, a more traditional poem in that the images belong
together chronologically and spatially as well as logically. The poem is a
winter landscape, a snowscape, composed of its various natural elements as
seen by the poet-clown. The images slip from reality into surreality. The
poem opens with a striking image and with the only sound that animates an
otherwise moribund scene. The dog howling heavenwards simultaneously
stands for Man: the perverse, guilty, god-forsaken *Menschentier*. There is no
reason to suppose that Lichtenstein was familiar with the Jewish symbolism
of the dog as an unclean animal and therefore an emblem of the uncleanness
(*das Hündische*) in man, but the idea certainly fits. The wolf baying at the
moon is subsumed in the image, but, bearing Lichtenstein's city-dwellers in
mind, it is *homo homini lupus* that is the relevant *Reflexion* here. Finally the
image has a personal connotation; a year later Lichtenstein wrote, in two
lines ascribed to Kuno Kohn which are as personal as anything he ever
wrote:

> Wer sagt die Qual, wenn ich in der Nacht auf Straßen
> Nach dir zum toten Himmel schrie —
>
> (*GG* 82)

The dog is therefore also an emblem of longing and despair (*ich armer Hund*),
while the distant echo of Tasso points back to the poet's early reading of
Goethe; but what a profound gulf separates his work from Goethe's. No
doubt the sky does look like old grey stone, but the heavens are brought
down to earth by the simile. The dead, fishless river (now so commonplace)
looks like a line of tar on the snow. The second stanza is more surrealistic,

although the poetic logic is unexceptionable. Three tall pointed trees, presumably poplars and probably inspired by van Gogh, look like frozen flames; knife-like they stick up into the air in which 'ein Vogelfetzen einsam hängt' — it is as though the birds have been cut to shreds by the tree-knives, a grotesque image which points beyond the fact that few of summer's birds now remain to something far more sinister: the destruction or decreation of the natural world. The romantic imagination itself is in tatters. The world is fast returning to its orginal chaos. The movement of the observer's eye is transferred to the streetlamps which are seen as wading townwards through the snow. There is, finally, the only sign of man, who is a diminished presence in more senses than one, a figure stripped of all significance, analogous to the 'Vogelfetzen'.

Better known than 'Der Winter' is a similar poem, 'Nebel' (*GG* 59):

Ein Nebel hat die Welt so weich zerstört.
Blutlose Bäume lösen sich in Rauch.
Und Schatten schweben, wo man Schreie hört.
Brennende Biester schwinden hin wie Hauch.

Gefangne Fliegen sind die Gaslaternen.
Und jede flackert, daß sie noch entrinne.
Doch seitlich lauert glimmend hoch in Fernen
Der giftge Mond, die fette Nebelspinne.

Wir aber, die, verrucht, zum Tode taugen,
Zerschreiten knirschend diese wüste Pracht.
Und stechen stumm die weißen Elendsaugen
Wie Spieße in die aufgeschwollne Nacht.

However, despite some striking line-images ('Ein Nebel hat die Welt so weich zerstört'; 'Brennende Biester schwinden hin wie Hauch'; 'Gefangne Fliegen sind die Gaslaternen'; 'Der giftge Mond, die fette Nebelspinne'), the poem is a relatively weak one thanks partly to the not wholly inspired choice of images (Lichtenstein's poetic method at this time is a hit-or-miss one), partly to the presence of enjambment, which means that the expressionistic line-by-line composition of 'Die Dämmerung' and 'Der Winter' is diluted and weakened by a conventional or prosy structure, and partly to the fact that the intended ambiguity of the poem gives way to obscurity. Of the four key lines it is the opening line that is the most successful of all; to write of the world being 'softly destroyed' is a highly effective way of expressing the blurring of outlines in fog. The last line of the first stanza is, I think, striking but unclear: one assumes that 'brennend' means 'sehnsüchtig', and that the 'Biester' are 'Menschenbiester', but this is only an assumption. The ambiguity of 'brennend' was hardly necessary. The two images in the second stanza are strikingly different in kind. To compare the sputtering gas-lamps to 'Gefangne Fliegen' is perhaps fanciful rather than whimsical. With 'Der giftge Mond, die fette Nebelspinne' it is a very different matter. Both the epithet 'giftig' and the spider-image derive from the greenish moon whose shafts of light half-penetrate the fog, but the image, reminiscent of Odilon Redon, both shows an altogether higher order of imagination at work and is surreally ominous. It is not an image that is easily forgotten. The poem ends, as Lichtenstein's poems not infrequently do, with an expression of man's helplessness and misery when faced, in this case, with what in retrospect seems to be the fog of human ignorance of the meaning of life. The poem is accordingly much more than the 'Darstellung der Nebelstimmung durch Aufzählung der Nebelphänomene' for which Clemens Heselhaus mistook it.[32]

The poems of *Die Dämmerung* are basically urban poems, poems about the modern monster city which so obsessed Lichtenstein's contemporaries Heym, Hoddis, Benn and Trakl. Klaus Kanzog has well said that:

> Lichtensteins Ausdruckswelt wird bestimmt durch das Erlebnis der Großstadt und eine Reihe immer wiederkehrender Motive. Straßen, Häuser, Rummelplätze, Kneipen kontrastieren mit Landschaftserinnerungen und entwickeln sich zu Zwangsvorstellungen. Einsamkeit, Sehnsucht, Prostitution und Tod sind zentrale Begriffe, die trotz des Caféhauscharakters vieler Gedichte einen echten Lebenskonflikt sichtbar machen. (In: *GG* 103)

What is important, however, is how this urban environment is expressed. It is through the imagery that Lichtenstein's city experience is rendered; as Heselhaus has said, 'Das Verfahren ist das der Metaphorisierung'.[33] This applies both to the poetry and to the prose sketches, as even a few examples reveal: 'Laternen waren düstere Sumpfblumen, die auf schwärzlich glimmenden Stielen flackerten' (*GP* 62; cf. *GG* 68 'Die Sonne, eine Butterblume, wiegt sich / Auf einem Schornstein, ihrem schlanken Stiele'), 'Lampen, die Blumen der Nacht, glimmen' (*GP* 94), 'Er sank hinunter. Tief, tief in einem Schlaf hinein wie in einen Sarg aus sanften Frauen' (*GP* 96), 'Augen und Sehnsucht: Schwarze Flammen aus dem Gesicht beleuchten die weiße Stirn, hinter der tausend mit Sehnsucht gefärbte Bilder funkeln' (*GP* 96). Such images show that Lichtenstein anticipated the surrealism of Yvan Goll by some years.

His view of the city which both fascinated and repelled him is made clear when he apostrophizes Berlin: 'Berlin, du bunter Stein, du Biest' (*GG* 91), 'Du, mein Berlin, du Opiumrausch, du Luder' (*GG* 92). In the poet's mind the sheer concrete, physical reality of the city fused with a surreal vision which mythologized city and inhabitants alike. The figures that he sees around him include: 'verträumte Polizisten' (*GG* 44), 'zerbrochne Bettler' (*GG* 44), 'wehleidge Kater' (*GG* 44), 'verlauste Burschen' (*GG* 45), 'verrauchte Krämer' (*GG* 45), 'Menschenbiester' (*GG* 46), 'sehnsüchtge Sünder' (*GG* 48) and 'bemalte Weiber' (*GG* 51). Many of Lichtenstein's past-participial adjectives point to the corrupting influence of the city.

Significantly, these figures all date from the twelve months following 'Die Dämmerung', after which they disappear. The lurid, grotesque, surrealistic imagery as such is found almost exclusively in poems of the 'Dämmerung' type, on which he presently turned his back altogether in favour of a more sobre, realistic form of poetry.

The city peopled by such figures is composed of 'Häuser wie Särge' (*GG* 46), of 'Häuserrudel' (*GG* 52: the *homo homini lupus* theme again), houses which he declares to be 'halbtote alte Leute' (*GG* 60). Of the streets he writes: 'Wie alte Knochen liegen . . . die verfluchten Straßen da' (*GG* 65). The human animal has made his city into a contagion of the once-natural world. Trees are 'zerlumpt' (*GG* 46), fields 'betrunken' (*GG* 46); even the winds are 'magre Hunde' (*GG* 60; cf. *GP* 55: 'Manchmal kam ein Wind, ein giftiger heißer Hund'. The starting-point for the metaphor was presumably the word *Windhund*). The very heavens are corrupted by man's animality: the sky is a 'blaue Sau' (*GG* 92). This is the most surreal of the many memorable sky-images in his work of the years 1911-1913; others include: 'Und über allem hängt ein alter Lappen — / Der Himmel . . . heidenhaft und ohne Sinn' (*GG* 46. Was his starting-point the German flag?), 'Der Himmel ist verheult und melancholisch' (*GG* 51), 'Der Himmel ist ein graues Packpapier, / Auf dem die Sonne klebt — ein Butterfleck' (*GG* 65), 'Himmel klebt an Städten wie ein Gas' (*GG* 65), 'Der Himmel ist wie eine blaue Qualle' (*GG* 67), and 'Der Himmel ist ersoffen' (*GG* 68). In that corrupt sky there lurks 'Der giftige Mond, die fette Nebelspinne' (*GG* 59), while 'Die Sonne leckt mit heißem, giftgem Maul / Am Boden wie ein Hund' (*GG* 55). The picture that emerges, although a conflated one, accurately represents the poet in his 'Bilderbuch' phase (1911-13). What is so extrordinary about the poems in question is the fact that they implicitly reject the physical world while being themselves so exuberantly detailed, or, as Alfred Lemm put it: 'Am Rande radikalster Verneinung des Gestaltlichen durchschießt die Freude am Gestalten Ihre Gedichte und wird Ursache ihrer erstaunlichen Vollkommenheit und, gar nicht selten, verlockender Spielerei'.[34]

Any poet whose work may be supposed to be in some way extreme, is likely to find himself being guyed. This was the case with Lichtenstein. On 31 July 1912 Ernst Blass published in *Die Aktion* a platitudinous take-off of poems like 'Die Dämmerung', entitled 'Nehmen Se jrotesk — det hebt Ihnen':

Ein alter Mensch trinkt eine 'Weiße mit'.
Die Sonne glotzt laut und unablässig.
Vier Leute kommen heim von einem Ritt.
Ein Kritiker wird plötzlich sehr gehässig.

Betthasen schwirren schweinisch, aber nett.
Ein Oberlehrer kauft sich einen Kragen,

Er hat den alten nun genung getragen.
Ein flacher Neger starrt in die 'B.Z.'.
Der Himmel hängt wie eine Dyspepsie
Herab auf Wilmersdorf, die Dichterstadt.
Ein Puter putert sich verzerrt und matt.
Und eine Henne ruft: Kikeriki.

Blass's parody is itself the subject of a fragment from the first version of Lichtenstein's sketch 'Café Klößchen', which was first published in his posthumous *Gedichte und Geschichten* (Vol. 2: *Geschichten*) in 1919. The main part of the fragment is as follows:

> In der Nähe Kohns sprachen im Kreise wenig bekannte Kritiker, Maler, Dichter und ein paar. Zumeist Mitarbeiter der neuen Zeitschrift: 'Das andere A' und der unregelmäßig von dem kleinen begeisterten Lutz Laus für die Hebung der Unsittlichkeit angefertigten Monatsschrift: 'Der Dackel' . . .
>   Man stritt sich gerade um den literarischen Unwert des Herrn Kohn. Der Dichter Gottschalk Schulz, ein Jurist, erklärte, ihm sei unbegreiflich, daß Herr Doktor Bryller den Kohn lobe. Kohn schildere alles anders. Kohn sei ein Lügner. Kohn sei grotesk. — Der begabte Doktor Berthold Bryller sagte darauf: 'Grotesk sein, sei kein Nachteil. Groteske sei immerhin eine Brücke zu einem Weg.' Und ein Witzblattredakteur, der eigentlich nicht hierher gehörte, schrie schüchtern: 'Auch ich schätze alles, was grotesk und originell ist und über den stumpfsinnigen deutschen Tintensumpf hinausstrebt.' — Aber Lutz Laus rief: 'Ich schätze gar nichts. Ich teile diese Knaben ein in Burschen, welche schreiben, weil ihnen nichts einfällt, und in Gesindel, welches schmiert, weil ihm so zumute ist.' — Spinoza Spaß, ein Gymnasiast, der dämlich an einem Stuhle hing, freute sich langsam. Er blickte boshaft zu dem einsamen Kohn. Und sagte, weiches Gemüt und heimatlichen Akzent durch Berlinern etwas verbergend: 'Nehmen Se jrotesk, det hebt Ihnen.' — Alle lachten. (*GP* 63)

For the sketch to be appreciated, the following approximate identifications need to be known, although any connexion with reality is fairly fortuitous: 'Das andere A' = *Die Aktion;* Lutz Laus = Karl Kraus; 'Der Dackel' = *Die Fackel;* Gottschalk Schulz = Georg Heym; Doktor Berthold Bryller = Kurt Hiller; ein Witzblattredakteur = Peter Scher, editor of *Simplicissimus;* Tintensumpf = a reference to Peter Scher's *Unkenrufe aus dem Tümpel der Kultur* (1910); Spinoza Spaß = Ernst Blass. What is most important, however, is the fact that Kuno Kohn is a *persona* of Alfred Lichtenstein. It is time that we considered this genial dwarf in more detail.

The paper cover of Lichtenstein's first collection, *Die Dämmerung* (1912), carried a drawing of *Frau Welt* in the form of a sphinx. In Kuno Kohn's 'Marienlieder' the name Maria is given to *Frau Welt*. 'Weib ist nur ein Vorwand für namenlose Sehnsucht', we read in one of Lichtenstein's prose fragments (*GP* 95); this romantic *Sehnsucht,* which is generally ironized by being attributed to the unromantic-looking 'Kuno Kohn', is a fundamental feature of Alfred Lichtenstein's attitude to life, just as fundamental as the more obvious despair which is often expressed through a devil-may-care nonchalance. Rene Schickele described Lichtenstein as a 'schwermütiger

Exzentriker', but it is to Lichtenstein's own description of his *persona*, the clown Kuno Kohn, as 'urkomisch ernst, verrückt', that one returns again and again, for this is a description of the poet himself, whose *Verrücktheit*, which he continually stresses, consists partly in this same nonchalance, and partly in his 'crazy' imagination, which was as remarkable as Heym's, in quite a different way; Kuno Kohn is told by Max Mechenmal (= Jakob van Hoddis): 'Aber du hast doch komische Einfälle. Das ist doch verrückt' (*GP* 41).

Lichtenstein wrote some of his poems in the *persona* of Kuno Kohn ('Lied der Sehnsucht des Kuno Kohn', 'Die fünf Marienlieder des Kuno Kohn', etc.). In other poems and in many of the prose sketches he simultaneously guyed and revealed himself in the guise of Kuno Kohn (we have seen that his literary friends and acquaintances were similarly mocked). Kuno Kohn, who made his début in a sketch bearing his name (first published in *Der Sturm* on 6 October 1910) is a weird figure:

> Kuno Kohn ist häßlich, er hat einen Buckel. Das Haar ist messingfarben, das Gesicht ist bartlos und von Furchen rissig. Die Augen sehen alt aus, um sie sind Schatten. Am Hals. beginnt ein Narbe wie ein Regenrinne. Das eine Bein ist angeschwollen. (*GP* 12)

The life which Lichtenstein ascribes to Kuno is no less grotesque, for he makes him the adopted son of a widowed prison chaplain who rejoices in the ambivalent name of Christian Kohn. Kuno's early life is not propitious; but it is — presumably — symbolical: 'Kuno Kohn verbrachte die erste halbwache Jugend in den trostlosen steinernen Räumen und Höfen des Zuchthauses' (*GP* 83). This is an oblique reference to Lichtenstein's own earliest experience of the Berlin by which he was captivated. Kuno shares his creator's anxieties:

> Blieb immer zwerghaft. Blaß und verträumt schlich er einher. Verschüchtert und furchtsam . . . das Nebensächlichste hatte Bedeutung, entsetzte ihn. Überall und von allem fürchtete er Unheil . . . Die großen Probleme, die den Kuno Kohn, sobald er einigermaßen denken konnte, immer wieder quälten, waren hauptsächlich Tod und Gott . . . Allmählich mehrten sich die Zweifel. Er mußte an seinen Tod glauben und den Glauben an Gott verlassen. Als er in die Schule kam, begann die Fülle von Leiden, die für manche Kinder damit verbunden sind. (*GP* 84ff.)

The great day of Kuno's life comes when he receives an invitation to read some of his poems at a meeting of the 'Klub Clou' presided over by 'Doktor Bryller'. The reading is a success; it is also a case of wishful thinking, for it appears that Lichtenstein himself was not even invited to read his work at Kurt Hiller's 'Cabaret Gnu'. As a result, Kuno becomes a habitué of the 'Café Klößchen', although he did not belong to the 'Klößchenclique' proper since he was on bad terms with most of the literary gentlemen in question (*GP* 64), a reference to Lichtenstein's relations with Georg Heym, Jakob van Hoddis, Ernst Blass and other members of the group of writers who used to meet in the Café des Westens (popularly known as the 'Café Größenwahn'). A further highlight of Kuno's life is his affair with Gottschalk Schulz's girlfriend, Lisel Liblichlein, whose name points to two women in Lichtenstein's literary and private life: Lene Levi and Lili Lubasch. The relationship with Schulz probably reflects Lichtenstein's wish to get even with Georg Heym, who treated him with a good deal less than respect. More importantly, Lisel Liblichlein's name points straight back to Alfred Lichtenstein's own name, which makes it likely that here too wishful thinking is at work, and that she is a personification of Kuno's and Lichtenstein's own *Sehnsucht* ('Weib ist nur ein Vorwand für namenlose Sehnsucht': *GP* 95).

Kuno Kohn has, I think, been well described by Joachim Schreck as 'das Porträt seiner [Lichtenstein's] Doppelexistenz, das Porträt seines anderen Ich', 'Gegenpol einer inneren Spannung des Dichters', 'die groteske Variante des Dichters Alfred Lichtenstein.'[35] Kuno Kohn relates to Lichtenstein in much the same way as the 'mad' musician Johannes Kreisler related to his creator, Hoffmann. Kuno's physical appearance recalls Hoffmann's Klein Zaches and points forward to the figure for which he provided the model: Günter Grass's Oskar Matzerath.

The extraordinary thing about the Kuno Kohn poems is that they are among the most *personal* that Lichtenstein ever wrote. He is never more serious than when writing in the *persona* of, or writing about himself in the guise of 'Kuno Kohn', never more serious than when he seems most obviously to be clowning. His despairing view of life is expressed not *in propria persona*, but by his *alter ego*, Kuno Kohn; and if there is a degree of self-ironization, self-mockery and self-deflation involved in this indirect form of self-expression, there can be not the slightest doubt that the poet is being deadly serious when he makes Kuno say:

> Wie drollig ist . . . das Dasein. Und da lehnt man nun; irgendwo; irgendwie; ohne Beziehung; ganz belanglos; könnte ebenso gut, ebenso schlecht weiterschreiten; irgendwohin. Das macht mich unglücklich . . . Ein Suchen ohne Ziel . . . Ein Haltloser . . . Unbekannt mit allem . . . Man hat eine furchtbare Sehnsucht. O wüßte man wonach . . . Das Gefühl der vollkommenen Hilflosigkeit . . . habe ich häufig. Der einzige Trost ist: traurig sein. Wenn die Traurigkeit in Verzweiflung ausartet, soll man grotesk werden. Man soll spaßeshalber weiterleben. Soll versuchen, in der Erkenntnis, daß das Dasein aus lauter brutalen hundsgemeinen Scherzen besteht, Erhebung zu finden. (*GP* 53f, 61)

Lichtenstein's despair, so memorably voiced by Kuno, is part of his basic romanticism. He may belong among the urban poets of early expressionism in the sense that many of his most characteristic poems are ironical cityscapes, but he longed to escape from this latterday Babylon back into the remembered magic of childhood; this is shown by 'Rückkehr des Dorfjungen' (8.5.1913: *GG* 67), where the poet's tragic disillusionment is seen in the way in which the 'große grüne Wiese' of his childhood world turned into 'Die grüne Leiche der verlornen Welt' (*GG* 73). Symbol of this magical other order is the summer sky, which he describes as 'der schöne

blaue / Ewige Himmel' (*GG* 67): 'Ein weißer Vogel ist der große Himmel'
(*GG* 60). The most explicit expression of this comes in the first two stanzas
of 'Der Gerührte' (4.11.1912: *GG* 79), which in turn brings us to one of the
best and most characteristic of his early poems, 'Fern':

Ich möchte in Nacht mich bergen,
Nackt und scheu,
Und um die Glieder Dunkelheit decken
Und warmen Glanz . . .
Ich möchte weit hinter die Hügel der Erde wandern —

Tief hinter die gleitenden Meere,
Vorbei den singenden Winden . . .
Dort treff ich die stillen Sterne,
Die tragen den Raum durch die Zeit
Und wohnen am Tode des Seins,
Und zwischen ihnen sind graue,
Einsame Dinge . . .
Welke Bewegung vielleicht
Von Welten, die lange verwesten —
Verlorener Laut —
Wer will das wissen . . .
Mein blinder Traum wacht fern den Wünschen der Erde.

(*GG* 16. The punctuation is original;
there are no omissions)

If 'Fern' had been written a little later, the diction might well have been less,
the structure more conventionally poetic; what is certain is that such an
openly romantic and personal piece would have been distanced by being
ascribed to the crazy dwarf, Kuno Kohn, whose feelings, as we have seen,
were the same as those expressed here. Lichtenstein is no simple romantic;
he is a romantic whose attitude to himself and to his own romanticism is
ironical or knowing. He is a complex, divided personality, whose sphere is
tragicomedy. This is why the sky not only stands for the world of magic, of
the dream, but may also stand for the never-never land of adulthood and
indeed for the brutality of life with its unrealized dreams. A striking poem,
'Der Ausflug', written on 3 July 1912, starts as a poem about escape from
the crassness of city life, but ends as a poem about man's helplessness in the
face of nature:

Du, ich halte diese festen
Stuben und die dürren Straßen
Und die rote Häusersonne,
Die verruchte Unlust aller
Längst schon abgeblickten Bücher
Nicht mehr aus.

Komm, wir müssen von der Stadt

Weit hinweg.
Wollen uns in eine sanfte
Wiese legen.
Werden drohend und so hilflos
Gegen den unsinnig großen,
Tödlich blauen, blanken Himmel
Die entfleischten, dumpfen Augen,
Die verwunschnen,
Und verheulte Hände heben.

(*GG* 53)

This is surely the most terrible of Lichtenstein's premonitory or precognitive poems, for the final image points forward to the scene just over two years later when the poet lay dying in the countryside outside Rheims. No doubt the sky looked as indifferent as ever.

The other interesting group of poems in the 'Dämmerung' section of Lichtenstein's collected poems are the prophetic poems which point forward both to his final style and to his final fate. The first of these, 'Prophezeiung', is in part a summation of his city-poetry:

Einmal kommt — ich habe Zeichen —
Sterbesturm aus fernem Norden.
Überall stinkt es nach Leichen.
Es beginnt das große Morden.

(*GG* 62)

The form is familiar, although there is one significant change: the iambic pentameters have given way to a 4-beat line that points forward to the *Heine-Strophen* of his last poems. As one would expect, the imagery also reaches a climax here. Whereas Lichtenstein previously wrote of 'eine morsche Frau' (*GG* 52), we have now reached the stage where 'Alles nimmt sein ekles Ende', so that 'Mädchen platzen'. The signs of an impending catastrophe are unmistakable. In another poem, 'Die Zeichen', he lists them, doing so in a surprisingly playful way which is reminiscent of Hans Arp, whose early word-configurations were appearing in *Der Sturm* at this time:

Die Stunde rückt vor.
Der Maulwurf zieht um.
Der Mond tritt wütend hervor.
Das Meer stürzt um.

(*GG* 72)

The prophecies reach their sharpest and most poetic point when they become personal. More impressive as a poem than either 'Prophezeiung' or 'Die Zeichen' is 'Punkt':

Die wüsten Straßen fließen lichterloh
Durch den erloschnen Kopf. Und tun mir weh.
Ich fühle deutlich, daß ich bald vergeh —
Dornrosen meines Fleisches, stecht nicht so.
Die Nacht verschimmelt. Giflaternenschein
Hat, kriechend, sie mit grünem Dreck beschmiert.
Das Herz ist wie ein Sack. Das Blut erfriert.
Die Welt fällt um. Die Augen stürzen ein.

(*GG* 69)

'Punkt' was to be a turning-point for two reasons: because after it
Lichtenstein wrote hardly any more 'Dämmerung'-type poems, and because it was the last poem he wrote before he began the military service
which ended in his death.

Towards a New Realism

Once he had proved to himself that he could produce consistently good
poems in the style of 'Die Dämmerung', Lichtenstein moved on. In his late
poetry he leaves behind the 'groteskes Stimmungsgedicht' with its surrealistic imagery, and moves back to a simpler, more realistic form of
poetry. It seems that he too, like Heym, was moving away from the poetry of
the *Kaffeehaus*. He no longer hides behind his *persona*, but now writes openly
in the manner of Kuno Kohn. The poet has grown up, self and anti-self have
merged. It is no chance that his very last poem is written in the *Heine-
Strophen* which are otherwise characteristic mainly of his early work, for in
returning to Heine he was returning to his own roots.

Typical of the last year of Lichtenstein's life are relatively straight,
realistic, personal poems written in forms (*Heine-Strophe;* various cabaret
styles, including the *Couplet*) that go back to before *Die Dämmerung:* the
'Soldatengedichte' and 'Kriegsgedichte'. There is, of course, clowning
involved in writing army poems and even war-poems in a music-hall style;
but the clowning is serious, as it ultimately always is. Like the war-poems,
then, the army poems, which were written between January and July 1914,
are not a type of poem, but a group of poems of several different kinds.

The first two 'Soldatengedichte' — 'Einsamer Wächter' (*GG* 88) and
'Der Sohn' (*GG* 85) — are simple, realistic, conventional, sentimental
poems addressed by the lonely young recruit to his mother; they are written
in a kind of *Heine-Strophe*, but lack the sophistication of Heine. More subtle is
the first of the five 'Soldatenlieder', written on 13 May 1914 (*GG* 88), which
at first sight looks like a cabaret-ballad on the lines of the earlier 'Der
Barbier des Hugo von Hofmannsthal' (*GG* 25f.), although appearances are

deceptive. What matters are the discordances of the poem: the lack of the rhyme that the form leads one to expect, the occasional breaks in the iambic pentameter pattern, the contrast between what is said and what is meant, the contrast between the beginning of the poem ('Gut ist und schön, ein Jahr Soldat zu sein. / Man lebt so länger. Und man freut sich doch / Mit jedem Funken Zeit, den man dem Tod entreißt') and the ending ('O, der Gestank in einer Marschkolonne. / O, Laufschritt über holdes Frühlingsland.'). Despite its form, the poem is reminiscent of, and worthy of, Heine. Irony is everything, so that by the end the opening sentiments (given the lie by the Latin tag which they only partially render: *dulce et decorum est, pro patria mori*) have been destroyed by ridicule.

If 'Soldatenlieder, I' points forward to Lichtenstein's war-poems in its irony, its form (cf. 'Gebet vor der Schlacht'), and its sentiments, much the same is true of another poem written a few days later, 'Ein Generalleutnant singt':

Ich bin der Herr Divisionskommandeur,
Seine Exzellenz.
Ich habe erreicht, was menschenmöglich ist . . .
Wäre doch endlich ein Krieg
Mit blutigen, brüllenden Winden.
Das gewöhnliche Leben
Hat für mich keine Reize.

(*GG* 30)

Unaccountably grouped by Kanzog among what he called 'Capriccio'-type poems, 'Ein Generalleutnant singt' clearly belongs among the 'Soldatengedichte'; it also points forward to Lichtenstein's war-poems, and invites comparison with Siegfried Sassoon's 'The General'.

By the end of his year in the army, Lichtenstein seems to have been tolerated as the clown that he was:

Jetzt tut man mir nichts mehr beim Militär.
Wer achtet noch auf mich. Man hat sich längst gewöhnt
An meine sonderbaren Zivilistenaugen.
Beim Exerzieren bin ich halb im Traum
Und auf den Märschen mache ich Gedichte.

(*GG* 93)

That understated 'mehr' in the first line, combined with his silence in autumn 1913, suggest that initially he had a tough time of it in the army. It could not have been otherwise. In 'Abschied', a poem written when he was on pre-release leave in Salzburg, he began by echoing the opening line of 'Soldatenlieder, I':

Wohl war ganz schön, ein Jahr Soldat zu sein.
Doch schöner ist, sich wieder frei zu fühlen.

> Es gab genug Verkommenheit und Pein
> In diesen umbarmherzgen Menschenmühlen.

(*GG* 94)

The second line of the poem, however, confirms our reading of that earlier poem, while the third and fourth lines make it abundantly clear that for all his brave front, the poet in fact loathed and detested the army and all its works. Whatever about Alfred Lichtenstein, Kuno was no Prussian. Structurally 'Abschied' is a throw-back to the poems of *Die Dämmerung,* but the grotesqueries have now given way to a realism and a clarity in which Kuno Kohn and Alfred Lichtenstein speak with one voice. The tragic irony of the poem speaks for itself: within one month Lichtenstein had been recalled to the colours, and within a further two months he was dead. Fate, it seems, took him at his word.

The 'Soldatengedichte' illustrate Lichtenstein's ironical and then openly hostile attitude towards all things military. One of the most remarkable of them, a fragmentary poem beginning 'Doch kommt ein Krieg', shows that he had no illusions about the nature of the coming war:

> Doch kommt ein Krieg. Zu lange war schon Frieden.
> Dann ist der Spaß vorbei. Trompeten kreischen
> Dir tief ins Herz. Und alle Nächte brennen.
> Du frierst in Zelten. Dir ist heiß. Du hungerst.
> Ertrinkst. Zerknallst. Verblutest. Äcker röcheln.
> Kirchtürme stürzen. Fernen sind in Flammen.
> Die Winde zucken. Große Städte krachen.
> Am Horizont steht der Kanonendonner.
> Rings aus den Hügeln steigt ein weißer Dampf
> Und dir zu Häupten platzen die Granaten.

(*GG* 93)

These lines, written on 9/10 July 1914, a fortnight after the assassination of Archduke Franz Ferdinand and his wife, show that Lichtenstein was not among those who thought that the war would be a piece of cake; he — almost uniquely on the German side — had no vision of national or personal glory; he left that to divisional commanders and suchlike cattle. How could the man who only two weeks previously had written of his 'sonderbare Zivilistenaugen', see glory in war? Clearly he could not. Lichtenstein saw everything with the comic and therefore belittling vision of the satirist. His view of the war is accordingly an 'eccentric' one. He would have been constitutionally incapable of writing most of the outbreak-of-war poems. 'Doch kommt ein Krieg' is written in low-key iambic pentameters again; there are no end-rhymes, for even the thought of war follows no orderly pattern; but there are sufficient internal rhymes to hold the poem together. Man — the poet himself — is threatened as well as ridiculed by the halo of bursting shells around his head at the end of this poem which strangely anticipates the front-line poems that Lichtenstein was soon to be writing. Word-images like 'Zerknallst' and 'Verblutest' are in line with his curiously refracted vision, for he implies that there is something rather remiss about allowing oneself to blow up or bleed to death; but there is a sharp, mordant edge to his humour here.

Following the Declaration and mobilization, Lichtenstein was sent to the Western Front with his regiment on 8 August. Before leaving for the front he wrote the poem 'Abschied', which appeared in A.R. Meyer's pamphlet collection *Der Krieg. Ein Flugblatt* (1914). This so-called patriotic work was banned on account of Rudolf Leonhard's poem 'Franctireurs'; in retrospect it is obvious that it is Lichtenstein's that is the most realistic or honest contribution. 'Abschied' is a remarkable poem and a unique one:

Vorm Sterben mache ich noch mein Gedicht.
Still, Kameraden, stört mich nicht.

Wir ziehn zum Krieg. Der Tod ist unser Kitt.
O, heulte mir doch die Geliebte nit.

Was liegt an mir. Ich gehe gerne ein.
Die Mutter weint. Man muß aus Eisen sein.

Die Sonne fällt zum Horizont hinab.
Bald wirft man mich ins milde Massengrab.

Am Himmel brennt das brave Abendrot.
Vielleicht bin ich in dreizehn Tagen tot.

(*GG* 96)

The simple, naive, honest rhyming-couplet form contrasts with the bombast of most similar poems. The form, the wording (e.g. that initial 'mach ich noch mein Gedicht'), colloquialism (e.g. 'nit') and trite epithet and phrase ('das brave Abendrot', 'Die Sonne fällt zum Horizont hinab') are all deliberately un-'poetic'; Lichtenstein presumably feels that high-key poetry at this point would involve the falsification of emotion. Its very simplicity is the making of his poem. There are more rousing poems written in the first week of August 1914, but there is none more impressive in its realism. Clearly Lichtenstein kept his head when others all around were losing theirs. His final forecast was wrong, though: it was to be seven weeks, rather than two, before he was dead.

The next poem, 'Romantische Fahrt' (*GG* 96) is remarkable for the picture of Kuno sitting on top of an ammunition wagon rumbling through the countryside of this ironically named 'romantic journey', which shows Lichtenstein still refusing to take himself seriously. He must have been one of the few men in Europe to do so. He retains the satirist's distance, even when writing about himself; I know of no more memorable picture of a poet going to war than this:

Hoch auf dem kippligsten Patronenwagen sitzt
Wie eine kleine Unke, fein geschnitzt
Aus schwarzem Holz, die Hände weich geballt,
Am Rücken das Gewehr, sanft umgeschnallt,
Die rauchende Zigarre in dem schiefen Mund,
Faul wie ein Mönch, sehnsüchtig wie ein Hund,
— Baldriantropfen hat er an das Herz gedrückt —
Im gelben Mond urkomisch ernst, verrückt:
Kuno.

That the poet knew that he was going to his death is implied by the epithet
'romantic'. Lichtenstein's description of his *persona*, Kuno, as 'Faul wie ein
Mönch' recalls Baudelaire's description of himself as 'le mauvais moine'.
'Romantische Fahrt' and another, weaker poem, 'Kriegers Sehnsucht' (*GG*
97: it follows the pattern of the two early 'Soldatengedichte' to his mother),
were written as his regiment moved forwards on 10th-13th August. The
regimental historian reported that as the regiment moved forwards,
'Nerven und Phantasie wurden durch die neuen Eindrücke, die auf uns
einstürmten, gewaltig angespannt',[36] but his comment seems quite
irrelevant to Lichtenstein, whose attitude remains cool and laconic
throughout.

It was his remarkable objectivity which enabled him to write a poem that
would have created an uproar if it had been published at the time: 'Gebet
vor der Schlacht' (*GG* 97f.). The battle to which the title refers is the first
large-scale infantry engagement of the war, which took place on 14 August
1914. With the exception of the first and last lines, 'Gebet vor der Schlacht'
is written in trochaic tetrameters; it consists of a song said to be sung, *sotto
voce*, by every member of Lichtenstein's unit. The song takes the form of a
hilariously funny and totally unheroic prayer. The first stanza has an
ending worthy of Heine:

Inbrünstig singt die Mannschaft, jeder für sich:
Gott, behüte mich vor Unglück,
Vater, Sohn und heilger Geist,
Daß mich nicht Granaten treffen,
Daß die Luder, unsre Feinde,
Mich nicht fangen, nicht erschießen,
Daß ich nicht wie'n Hund verrecke
Für das teure Vaterland.

The ending of this stanza reveals what underlies the whole poem: the utter
disparity between what the poet makes his comrades pray, and what the
popular ideal of glory demands. The ideals of patriotism and heroism, of
sacrificing oneself on the altar of the fatherland, are mocked and debunked
by the simple ('cowardly') self-interest of the men. This is a remarkable

poem to have been written in August 1914, for it was not really until after the Battle of the Somme that the grandiose patriotic concepts began to be questioned and eventually replaced by other ideals. But Lichtenstein's poem not only mocks the heroic mode in general; it also parodies the expression of that mode in earlier battlefield-prayer poems. More particularly, Lichtenstein may well have had in mind two poems by Theodor Körner, 'Bundeslied vor der Schlacht' and 'Gebet während der Schlacht', which appeared, posthumously, in Körner's *Leyer und Schwert* (1814). 'Bundeslied vor der Schacht' was written on 12 May 1813, on the eve of the battle of Danneberg. The fourth stanza gives the best brief idea of the poem as a whole:

> Nun, mit Gott! wir wollen's wagen,
>> Fest vereint dem Schicksal stehn,
> Unser Herz zum Altar tragen
> Und dem Tod entgegengehn.
> Vaterland! dir woll'n wir sterben,
>> Wie dein großes Wort gebeut!
> Unsre Lieben mögen's erben,
>> Was wir mit dem Blut befreit.
> Wachse, du Freiheit der deutschen Eichen,
> Wachse empor über unsere Leichen!
> Vaterland, höre den heiligen Eid!

These are the sentiments expressed in August 1914 by all too many poets, Lichtenstein being one of the few honourable exceptions. However, if Lichtenstein's tetrameters are reminiscent of 'Bundeslied vor der Schlacht', the more interesting comparison is with Körner's 'Gebet während der Schlacht', also dating from 1813, the fourth stanza of which reads:

> Vater du, segne mich!
> In deine Hand befehl' ich mein Leben,
> Du kannst es nehmen, du hast es gegeben;
> Zum Leben, zum Sterben segne mich!
> Vater, ich preise dich!

Lichtenstein's 'Gebet vor der Schlacht' takes its tetrameter form from 'Bundeslied vor der Schlacht', but essentially it is a parodistic inversion of 'Gebet während der Schlacht'. The whole point of Körner's poem is that he is willing to die if God wills it. Lichtenstein is not.

The second stanza of Lichtenstein's unheroic poem is devastatingly honest and funny, although one can imagine contemporary readers — particularly the armchair warriors — describing it in quite different terms, calling for the damn fellow to be horsewhipped:

> Sieh, ich möchte gern noch leben,
> Kühe melken, Mädchen stopfen

Und den Schuft, den Sepp, verprügeln,
Mich noch manches Mal besaufen
Bis zu meinem selgen Ende.
Sieh, ich bete gut und gerne
Täglich sieben Rosenkränze,
Wenn du, Gott, in deiner Gnade
Meinen Freund, den Huber oder
Meier, tötest, mich verschonst.

Of course such an attitude, which the poet presumably shared with the Bavarian comrades-in-arms whom he is satirizing, is selfish, cowardly, thoroughly deplorable; but it is also true to life, and, at a time when most poets and poetasters were busy riding a wave of euphoria, is refreshingly down-to-earth and frank.

The last stanza echoes the first in its shock-ending, and this time the ending is underlined by a change of rhythm:

Aber muß ich doch dran glauben,
Lass' mich nicht zu schwer verwunden.
Schick mir einen leichten Beinschuß,
Eine kleine Armverletzung,
Daß ich als ein Held zurückkehr,
Der etwas erzählen kann.

The last line underlines the whole point of the poem. In August 1914 the word 'Held' normally occurs in the context of 'Heldentod'; to be a 'hero' is almost by definition to be dead. Lichtenstein's ideal is the 'hero' who lives to tell the tale; survival is all. It is not that he was anything so grand as a 'pacifist', although his work does invite comparison with that of Hugo Ball; he was, simply, a realist, and that at a time when realism was practically unknown. 'Gebet vor der Schlacht' is, I think, a remarkable poem, one of the best and certainly the funniest of Lichtenstein's war-poems; it is totally and uproariously anti-heroic, and this on the eve of the first great infantry battle of the war.

Lichtenstein's war-poems reflect his idiosyncratic and ironical vision; war, for him, is an extension of the grotesqueness of life, the consummation of all his fears. Not all his war-poems are as good, or as funny, or as committed as 'Gebet vor der Schlacht'. Two poems which he sent home on 22 August, 'Die Granate' (*GG* 98) and 'Nach dem Gefecht' (*GG* 99), both of them written in the rhyming couplets of 'Abschied' (*GG* 96), are relative failures because in 'Die Granate' he allows himself no scope for the irony on which all his best poems depend and is too easily satisfied with mere description, while in 'Nach dem Gefecht' he seems to lack any clear intention.

This he certainly has in his last poem, 'Die Schlacht bei Saarburg'. Both the gap from 22 August to 16 September, when 'Die Schlacht bei Saarburg' was sent home, and the content of this last poem, which did not reach Franz Pfemfert until the end of October 1914, well after Lichtenstein's death, suggest that the poet was involved in heavy fighting at the Battle of Saarburg (the official German designation for the fighting in which Lichtenstein's unit was involved on 18-22 August 1914) and subsequently. Saarburg was evidently the baptism of fire which caused his attitude to war to lose its ironical distance:

Die Erde verschimmelt im Nebel.
Der Abend drückt wie Blei.
Rings reißt elektrisches Krachen
Und wimmernd bricht alles entzwei.

Wie schlechte Lumpen qualmen
Die Dörfer am Horizont.
Ich liege gottverlassen
In der knatternden Schützenfront.

Viel kupferne feindliche Vögelein
Surren um Herz und Hirn.
Ich stemme mich steil in das Graue
Und biete dem Tode die Stirn.

(*GG* 100)

Lichtenstein's real poetic kinship is here revealed, for 'Die Schlacht bei Saarburg' is written in *Heine-Strophen*. As with Heine, there is an alternation of feminine and masculine endings, with only the masculine endings rhyming. There is, therefore, not only the same ambiguity and discord as in Heine, but also the added perspective and depth that comes from the deliberate echo of Lichtenstein's great predecessor. The basic tension in the poem is between poet and reality, that is, war. The poem falls into two distinct halves: the first six lines describe external reality, while the last six are devoted to the poet's reaction to that overwhelmingly hostile reality. The tension between passive poet-victim and aggressive external event is hammered home in those alternating endings, but inevitably the distinction between the two is blurred, for what matters is how reality is seen by the poet and the effect it has on him.

Thus the very first line ostensibly describes the world, at dusk, 'mouldering' in mist, but that brave, odd epithet does not conceal the fact that it is the poet's sense of reality, even his grip on reality that is becoming blurred and loosened by the continuous fighting of 18-20 August. The oppressive sense of reality is expressed in the second line: 'Der Abend drückt wie Blei', with the word 'Blei' standing as a reminder that the poet has been under fire for three days. The third line compares the continuous shellfire to a violent thunderstorm, with the feminine endings suggesting that it becomes a storm in the mind, a brain-storm that reduces the poet to a whimpering, moaning wreck. This reading is reinforced by the ending of the poem.

The second stanza shows the effect of war on the man-made world and on one individual man. The physical wreckage of ruined villages reflects, echoes and helps to cause the way in which the poet is reduced to mental wreck. The poet lies there, god-forsaken ('My God, why hast Thou forsaken me': the Biblical question points to the extent of the poet's desolation), while the incessant, nagging machine-gun fire further aggravates his overwrought condition, bringing him to the point where his grip on reality is loosened. The image in the first half of the last stanza ('Viel kupferne feindliche Vögelein / Surren um Herz und Hirn') is not just an obvious poeticism, a simile for all the bullets and shells sawing their way through the air, and not just a typical piece of *grotesquerie;* the childish image shows, surely, that the poet's mind has — at least temporarily — gone. It is because he has reached the end of his tether and can take no more, that he ends by writing: 'Ich stemme mich steil in das Graue / Und biete dem Tode die Stirn.' There is nothing else left for him to do but surrender to death, as he did near Vermandovillers (re-taken by Wilfred Owen's regiment exactly four years later), just nine days after sending home this poem.

Read in this way, 'Die Schlacht bei Saarburg' can be seen to be the deepest and most personal of Lichtenstein's all too few war-poems. It is a poem which shows the inadequacy of Kanzog's comment that 'Die Kriegsgedichte versuchen keine neuen stilistischen Experimente, sie wirken wie Briefzeilen, die unter dem Eindruck der Ereignisse geschrieben wurden und die nicht mehr als Berichte sein wollen.' (*GG* 103). This comment applies only to Lichtenstein's weakest war-poems, which are merely descriptive. It is not true of the far stronger poems which go beyond description to render comment ('Abschied', 'Gebet vor der Schlacht', etc.). It is perhaps typical of Lichtenstein that he should have written war-poems of two such widely differing kinds and qualities; it is certainly a fact that he did so.

His few war poems make Lichtenstein one of the best and most original of the German war poets, for they are 'self-deprecating, bitter and funny',[37] qualities which otherwise are found only in the work of the pacifist satirists Hugo Ball and Kurt Tucholsky. Even in August 1914 he sees everything with the 'eccentric' or curiously refracted eye of the satirist or 'clown'. The pomposity, inflated rhetoric and martial short-sightedness of most of the verse written in the early months of the war were totally alien to him. His originality and importance are seen nowhere more clearly than in his war-poetry; it is this, above all else, that shows how much German poetry lost in him.

One of the major innovators of his generation, Lichtenstein might well have developed into a major poet if he had been given the chance to do so.

As it is, the variety of his work is greater and the pattern of its development more complex than has been thought. To say, as it is too often said, that he, unlike Heym, was not a 'Frühvollendeter', is a partial truth which ignores something more important: the fact that by 1914 he had not only written a series of *Zeilengedichte* which are among the major achievements of Expressionism in poetry, but had outgrown Expressionism — which was, after all, essentially a phase poets passed through — and was writing in a style which anticipated the anti-war satires of Kurt Tucholsky and the *Neue Sachlicheit* of the post-war era in general. His importance as a poet lies only partly in the fact that, together with Hoddis, he 'created a new genre of half-realist, half-surrealist *montage*',[38] although we have seen that he did this. More importantly, it is with Lichtenstein that *Neue Sachlichkeit* begins in the sense that with him German poetry finally begins to turn its back on romantic otherworldliness and, under the influence of Heine, to come down to earth. That he was at the same time a romantic, only serves to underline the parallel with Heine. Like Heine, he was a poet who could 'demolish at . . . polished ease / Philistia's pomp and art's pomposities!'[39] And that, in 1914, was something that poetry needed very badly indeed.

Notes

Abbreviations. Heym: the abbreviation *DuS* (= *Dichtungen und Schriften*) is used, except in the case of *Lyrik* and *Tagebücher* (which appear in Vols. 1 and 3 respectively), my numerous references to which are given in the most concisely informative form, e.g. *L* 342, *T* 27.9.11; in dates the order is British. Lichtenstein: *GG* stands for *Gesammelte Gedichte*, and *GP* for *Gesammelte Prosa*.

[1] Dmitri Merejkowski, *The Forerunner*, 1902, Book XII, Chapter XII.
[2] *Modern German Poetry 1910-1960*, ed. M. Hamburger & C. Middleton, 1962, xxvi.
[3] W.H. Sokel, *The Writer in Extremis*, Stanford, 1959, 98.
[4] ibid.
[5] ibid.
[6] In the *Nachwort* to his admirable Reclam edition of Heym's *Gedichte*.
[7] Arthur Symons, *Charles Baudelaire. A Study*, 1920, 23.
[8] Arthur Symons, *The Symbolist Movement in Literature*, 2nd edn, 1908, 65.
[9] ibid., 72.
[10] Baudelaire, *Selected Poems*, ed. Joanna Richardson, 1975, 18f.
[11] T.S. Eliot, in his essay entitled 'Baudelaire'.
[12] Arthur Symons, *Charles Baudelaire. A Study*, 1920, 37.
[13] Hamburg, 1967, 46f, 130f.
[14] *Dichtung und Dichter der Zeit*, Leipzig, 1911, 833 (only in this edition).
[15] G.-A. Aurier, *Oeuvres posthumes*, Paris, 1898, 261.
[16] See my forthcoming *The Expressionist Generation and van Gogh*.
[17] Ernst Blass, in *Expressionismus*, ed. P.Raabe, Olten & Freiburg i.B. 1965, 38.
[18] 'Ogling through Ice: The Sullen Lyricism of Georg Heym,' *Books Abroad*, Spring 1971, 233.
[19] ibid., 238.
[20] Hamburger and Middleton, *Modern German Poetry 1910-1960*, 1962, xxvii.
[21] P. Thomson, *The Grotesque in German Poetry 1880-1933*, Melbourne, 1975, 69-72.
[22] H. Rölleke, in *Expressionismus als Literatur*, ed. W. Rothe, Berlin & Munich, 1969, 356.
[23] Viereck, loc. cit., 240.
[24] ibid.
[25] *Pan*, 1914/15, 49f.
[26] Arthur Symons, *The Symbolist Movement in Literature*, 2nd edn, 1908, 102.
[27] Klaus Kanzog, in *GP* 102.
[28] Joachim Schreck, in his edition of Lichtenstein, *Die Dämmerung. Ausgewählte Gedichte*, Berlin, 1977, 110.
[29] Johannes R. Becher, *Das poetische Prinzip*, Berlin, 1957, 103f.
[30] Joachim Schreck, op. cit., 107f.
[31] Michael Hamburger, *Reason and Energy*, 1957, 223f.
[32] Clemens Heselhaus, *Deutsche Lyrik der Moderne*, Düsseldorf, 1961, 307.
[33] ibid., 306.
[34] *Die Weißen Blätter*, II/I, 1915, 807.
[35] Joachim Schreck, op. cit., 105f.
[36] Otto Staubwasser, *Das K.B.2. Infanterie-Regiment Kronprinz*, Munich, 1924, 18.
[37] *Modern German Poetry 1910-1960*, ed. M. Hamburger & C. Middleton, 1962, 406.
[38] ibid.
[39] Ezra Pound, in his *Personae* of 1919.

Bibliography

Primary:

Heym, G. *Der ewige Tag*, Berlin, 1911.

Umbra vitae, Berlin, 1912.

Dichtungen, ed. K. Pinthus & E. Loewenson, Munich, 1922.

Dichtungen und Schriften. Gesamtausgabe, ed. K.L. Schneider, 4 Vols, Hamburg, 1960-68.

Lichtenstein, A. *Die Dämmerung*, Berlin-Wilmersdorf, 1913.

Gedichte und Geschichten, ed. K. Lubasch, 2 Vols, Munich, 1919.

Gesammelte Gedichte, ed. K. Kanzog, Zürich, 1962.

Gesammelte Prosa, ed. K. Kanzog, Zürich, 1966.

Bridgwater, P. (Ed.) *The Poets of the Café des Westens*, Leicester, 1984 (contains all the main poems discussed here).

Secondary:

Bridgwater, P. *The German Poets of the First World War*, London, 1985.

Damann, G., Schneider, K.L., & Schöberl, J. *Georg Heyms Gedicht 'Der Krieg'*, Heidelberg, 1978

Greulich, H. *Georg Heym (1887-1912). Leben und Werk*, Berlin, 1931.

Hamburger, M. *Reason and Energy*, London, 1957.

Hamburger, M. & Middleton, C. (Eds.) *Modern German Poetry 1910-1960*, London, 1962.

Heckmann, H. 'Marginalien zu Lichtenstein', *Akzente*, 1955, 408-421.

Heselhaus, C. *Deutsche Lyrik der Moderne*, Düsseldorf, 1961.

Kanzog, K. 'Die Gedichthefte Alfred Lichtensteins,; *Jahrbuch der deutschen Schillergesellschaft*, 1961, 376-401.

Korte, H. *Georg Heym*, Stuttgart, 1982.

Küntzel, H. 'Alfred Lichtenstein,' in: *Expressionismus als Literatur*, ed. W. Rothe, Berne & Munich, 1969, 398-409.

Lemm, A. 'Abschied von Lichtenstein,' *Die Weißen Blätter*, 1915, 807f.

'Brief an Alfred Lichtenstein,' *Almanach der Neuen Jugend 1917*, 134f.

Lichtenstein, A. 'Die Verse des Alfred Lichtenstein,' *Die Aktion*, 4 Oct. 1913, 942ff.

Mautz, K. *Mythologie und Gesellschaft im Expressionismus. Die Dichtung Georg Heyms*, Frankfurt/M & Bonn, 1961.

Rölleke, H. *Die Stadt bei Stadler, Heym und Trakl*, Berlin, 1966.

'Georg Heym,' in: *Expressionismus als Literatur*, ed. W. Rothe, Berne & Munich, 1969, 354-373.

Regenberg, A. *Die Dichtung Georg Heyms und ihr Verhältnis zur Lyrik Charles Baudelaires und Arthur Rimbauds*, Diss. Munich, 1961.

Schiller, I.

L'Influence de Rimbaud et de Baudelaire dans la poésie préexpressioniste allemande, Diss. Paris, 1968.

Schneider, K.L.

Der bildhafte Ausdruck in den Dichtungen Georg Heyms, Georg Trakls und Ernst Stadlers, Heidelberg, 1954.

Zerbrochene Formen. Wort und Bild im Expressionismus, Hamburg, 1967.

Schneider, K.L. & Burckhardt, G. (Eds.)

Georg Heym: Dokumente zu seinem Leben und Werk, Hamburg, 1968 (= Heym, *Dichtungen und Schriften,* Vol. 6).

Schreck, J.

'Nachwort' to his edition of Alfred Lichtenstein, *Ausgewählte Gedichte,* Berlin & Weimar, 1977.

Thomson, P.

The Grotesque in German Poetry 1880-1933, Melbourne, 1975.